Cryptography for Payment Professionals

Although cryptography plays an essential part in most modern solutions, especially in payments, cryptographic algorithms remain a black box for most users of these tools. Just as a sane backend developer will not drill down into low-level disk access details of a server filesystem, payments professionals have enough things to worry about before they ever need to bother themselves with debugging an encrypted value or a message digest. However, at a certain point, an engineer faces the need to identify a problem with a particular algorithm or, perhaps, to create a testing tool that would simulate a counterpart in a protocol that involves encryption.

The world of cryptography has moved on with giant leaps. Available technical standards mention acronyms and link to more standards, some of which are very large while others are not available for free. After finding the standards for the algorithm, the specific mode of operation must also be identified. Most implementations use several cryptographic primitives—for example, key derivation with a block cipher, which produces a secret that is used together with a hash function and a double padding scheme to produce a digital signature of a base64-encoded value. Understanding this requires more sifting through online sources, more reading of platform and library documents, and finally, when some code can be written, there are very few test cases to validate it.

Cryptography for Payment Professionals is intended for technical people, preferably with some background in software engineering, who may need to deal with a cryptographic algorithm in the payments realm. It does not cover the payment technology in-depth, nor does it provide more than a brief overview of some regulations and security standards. Instead, it focuses on the cryptographic aspects of each field it mentions. Highlights include:

- Major cryptographic algorithms and the principles of their operation.
- Cryptographic aspects of card-present (e.g., magnetic stripe, EMV) and online (e.g., e-Commerce and 3DS 2.0) transactions.
- A detailed description of TDES DUKPT and AES DUKPT protocols, as well as an example implementation and test cases for both.

It is best if the reader understands programming, number and string representations in machine memory, and bit operations. Knowledge of C, Python, or Java may make the examples easier to read but this is not mandatory

Cryptography for Payment Professionals

Ilya Dubinsky

CRC Press
Taylor & Francis Group
Boca Raton London New York

CRC Press is an imprint of the
Taylor & Francis Group, an **informa** business

AN AUERBACH BOOK

First edition published 2023
by CRC Press
6000 Broken Sound Parkway NW, Suite 300, Boca Raton, FL 33487-2742

and by CRC Press
4 Park Square, Milton Park, Abingdon, Oxon, OX14 4RN

CRC Press is an imprint of Taylor & Francis Group, LLC

© 2023 Taylor & Francis Group, LLC

ISBN: 978-1-032-44274-7 (hbk)
ISBN: 978-1-032-44276-1 (pbk)
ISBN: 978-1-003-37136-6 (ebk)

DOI: 10.1201/9781003371366

Typeset in Nimbus Roman
by KnowledgeWorks Global Ltd.

Publisher's note: This book has been prepared from camera-ready copy provided by the authors.

Code related to the book is available at the author's GitHub site: https://github.com/ilya-dubinsky/cfpp

To Rabbeinu, Rajoub, Oren Guru,
and the dearest Mr. Carasso.

Gentlemen, splice the main brace!

Contents

Preface

It is hard to feel thrilled at the site of a new mandate letter from a card scheme or exhilarated by the fact that a new key representation method may become mandatory as soon as 2025. And the host-to-host PIN translation with a static key stays the same after you figure it out once.

Years spent working as the keeper of payments knowledge at a fast-growing, primarily e-Commerce acquirer can really dull one's sense of excitement.

Then the changes came. First, we had to handle the PSD2 regulation, and the EMV 3DS authentication protocol quickly became mandatory.

We grumbled about the copious extra work that landed on our lap. Little did we know how lucky we were.

EMV 3DS is a repeatable, transparent protocol with a clear message structure. An EMV 3DS message could be written into a log in case of an error, analyzed, and the error corrected. A transaction could be resent as many times as were needed in the testing environment. These traits are rarely treasured in a protocol, being taken for granted.

One day, after a strategic deal got signed, we had to get our hands dirty with some POS devices.

Suddenly, very repeatable, static, and simple things became much harder. If, before that, we could prepare fixed PIN blocks for each test card number, encipher them with a static key and keep reusing the values, with the new devices, there was no way around a dynamically generated PIN key derived from a value based on the device number.

Now, instead of simply saying "we will use DUKPT; we know it works," the algorithm's internals had to be explained to a developer so that a testing tool could be built. Once the tool was built, it had to be tested itself since, for some reason, it did not work correctly right away.

DUKPT generates some keys and encrypts some values with them. The cryptographic algorithms it uses are of the sound, strong kind, and one of the properties of a strong and sound cryptographic algorithm is that it is entirely impossible to tell what went wrong with it by looking at the output value.

No standard or book described each intermediate computation with the correct input and output values, so the code had to be traced step by step and triple-checked to ensure the algorithm was implemented correctly.

It turned out that, besides understanding how the method should work, it helps to understand why it succeeds. It also turned out that the test results and the carefully gathered website links should be best kept in one place because they will be needed again and again.

We found ourselves in need of a handy, easily accessible, and concise source of knowledge for cryptography in payments so that whenever some encryption results do not match (again!), an engineer could quickly find a detailed, step by step description of how the encryption should look like, perhaps pick up a code sample and a test case, and, if there are a few more minutes, also figure out what makes it work.

Writing a book seemed like a good idea at the time, and so here it is.

Author Biography

Ilya Dubinsky has 20 years of experience in the software industry. He is the VP of CTO Office in Finaro (formerly Credorax), the fastest-growing cross-border acquiring bank in the European Union. Ilya defines technological roadmap of the company, manages its IP portfolio and guides participation in international standard bodies. He also leads the in-house technology research, including in the fields of cryptography, blockchain, and AI. Ilya participates in global groups and bodies, including ISO, The Berlin Group banking industry standards initiative, the Payment Services User Group of Bank of Malta and the Fintech Forum of Bank of Israel. Capitalizing on his years of experience in software development, product and project management in Telecom and Finance industries, Ilya teaches a fin-tech class in Holon Institute of Technology and oversees joint research projects with Tel Aviv University.

List of Figures

Chapter 1

Building Blocks

1.1 How to Read This Book

Although cryptography plays an essential part in most modern solutions, especially in payments, cryptographic algorithms have been implemented in many libraries, frameworks, and even appliances and remain a black box for most users of these tools.

This attitude is well-justified: just as a sane backend developer will not drill down into low-level disk access details of a server filesystem, payments professionals have enough things to worry about before they ever need to bother themselves with debugging an encrypted value or a message digest.

However, at a certain point, an engineer faces the need to identify a problem with a particular algorithm or, perhaps, to create a testing tool that would simulate a counterpart in a protocol that involves encryption.

At this point, the engineer suddenly realizes that the world of cryptography has moved on with giant leaps since their college years. Available technical standards mention acronyms and link to more standards, some of which are very large while others are not available for free.

After finding the standards for the algorithm, the specific mode of operation must also be identified. Most implementations use several cryptographic primitives – for example, key derivation with a block cipher, which produces a secret that is used together with a hash function and a double padding scheme to produce a digital signature of a base64-encoded value. Understanding this requires

DOI: 10.1201/9781003371366-1

more sifting through online sources, more reading of platform and library documents, and finally, when some code can be written, there are very few test cases to validate it.

The book is intended for technical people, preferably with some background in software engineering, who may need to deal with a cryptographic algorithm in the payments realm in the future or present. It does not cover the payment technology in-depth, nor does it provide more than a brief overview of some regulations and security standards. Instead, it focuses on the cryptographic aspects of each field it mentions. It is best if the reader understands programming, number and string representations in machine memory, and bit operations. Knowledge of C, Python, or Java may make the examples easier to read but this is not mandatory.

The overview chapter on cryptography (*Section 1.3 Cryptography*) provides an introduction to the field and covers all significant algorithms used today in the industry. It is followed by an overview of the payment methods and the industry in *Chapter 2* Understanding Payments.

Several chapters cover *cryptography* in various technological areas of the payment field: first, the security of a payment card (*Chapter 3 Securing the Plastic: Magnetic Stripe and EMV*), then the network, the basis of all online payment methods (*Chapter 4 Securing the Network*).

Methods to protect the PIN are cryptography-heavy and merit a separate chapter, *Chapter 5 Protecting the PIN*.

Finally, regulatory aspects of cryptographic algorithms and requirements for key strength are addressed in *Chapter 6 Regulation and Compliance*.

Besides the theoretical descriptions, the book contains implementation examples of some necessary bitwise operations (see *Appendix A Bits and Digits*), basic and advanced cryptographic algorithms (*Appendix B Cryptographic Examples*), and step-by-step examples of some of the protocols mentioned in the book (*Appendix C EMV Examples, Appendix D PIN Examples*, and *Appendix E JOSE Examples*).

Source code for these examples, some test implementations, and test cases are available at `https://github.com/ilya-dubinsky/cfpp`. The repository has subfolders for the respective supported languages. References for each language are relative to the parent subfolder, so "a C example is found in `src/bits.c`" means that the file resides at `c/src/bits.c`.

1.2 Notations and Formats

Throughout the book, the following notations and formats are mentioned and used:

`0xN,` `0xNN` where N is 0 to 9 or 'A' to 'F,' is the value represented with the hexadecimal digits N or NN. A 4-bit value (nibble) is represented with a single digit, as 0xN, and an 8-bit value (byte) is represented with two digits, as 0xNN.

'AA' where AA are alphanumeric characters, is a string value in the ASCII encoding. For example, 'M8' corresponds to bytes 0x4D, 0x37.

~A bitwise NOT applied to the value A.

$A \ll n$ bitwise shift left of the value A by n bits.

$A \equiv B$ mod N integers A and B are congruent modulo the integer n. In other words, there exists an integer d such that $A - B = dN$.

A mod N the reduction of the integer A modulo N. In other words, the unique d for which there exists an integer r, $0 <= r < N$, such that $A = dn + r$.

$A \parallel B$ concatenation of the values A and B, seen as a sequence of bits.

$A \oplus B$ the XOR operation on values A and B.

A=B the A is assigned the value of B.

base64(A) Base64 encoding of the binary value A. Unless specified otherwise, the URL flavor of the Base64 encoding is used (see A.8).

BCD Binary-coded decimal. Refers to the representation of a decimal value in memory where each digit of the number is mapped to a nibble. For instance, the decimal value of 48is represented as 0x48 (while as a binary number, it is equal to 0x30).

byte 8-bit unit of information. The value for the byte is often shown as two hexadecimal digits.

$D(C) = M$ decryption of the ciphertext value C with the algorithm D yields the cleartext M.

$D_K(C) = M$ decryption of the ciphertext value C with the algorithm D yields the cleartext M.

$E(M) = C$ encryption of the cleartext value M with the algorithm E yields the ciphertext C.

$E_K(M) = C$ encryption of the cleartext value M with the algorithm E and the key K yields the ciphertext C.

leftmost most significant, if applied to bits.

nibble A 4-bit value corresponding to a single decimal digit. A byte consists of two nibbles, corresponding to 4 most significant and 4 less significant bits.

rightmost least significant, if applied to bits.

1.3 Cryptography

Cryptography is the art and science of secure communication in the presence of adversarial behavior.

The security of communication is typically divided into several separate functions, and, as we see later, all of those can be supported by a cryptographic algorithm or algorithms:

1. *Confidentiality* – a third party's inability to understand the message.

2. *Authentication* – a third party's inability to pose as the message sender.

3. *Integrity* – a third party's inability to modify the message in transit and remain undetected.

4. *Non-repudiation* – sender's inability to deny sending a message.

At this point, it is intuitively clear that all of these functions can be very useful in payments.

For example, it is essential not to let an eavesdropper intercept sensitive payment credentials such as a credit card number, which means maintaining the confidentiality of payment communications. It is crucial to ensure that the account owner is indeed the one making the payment (authentication) and that the owner cannot deny making the payment later (non-repudiation). Finally, it is essential to ensure the attacker did not modify the message in transit (integrity).

Surprisingly enough, practical cryptography can achieve all these goals with a relatively small number of building block algorithms combined skilfully into higher-level protocols. While a complete understanding of cryptography undoubtedly requires in-depth knowledge of the internals of each of those algorithms, their detailed description is beyond the scope of this book.

Many of these "primitive" individual functions are implemented as part of mature libraries, available on all major platforms and for all major technology stacks. Others are easy to develop as a straightforward combination of several standard functions.

For a practitioner, it is more important to understand which method to use, when, and how to invoke it on a particular technology platform than it is to know how exactly the implementation works.

1.3.1 Complexity and feasibility

One important principle must be well-understood to grasp the motivation behind many design decisions in cryptographic protocols and the accompanying procedures.

Modern cryptography uses extensive computations and, as such, relies on computing power. Any cryptographic method that is practically useful with computers theoretically be beaten with the *brute force* approach of trying all possible keys.

Consequently, there are no unbreakable cryptographic algorithms[1]; there only are algorithms that are either economically not feasible to break with *brute force* or algorithms for which there is not nearly enough computing power in the world available to break them. The terms *computationally hard* or just *hard* are used to reflect the lack of computing capacity. For brevity, we will sometimes use "impossible" in the meaning of "computationally hard."

Suppose a particular algorithm can be broken significantly faster than with brute force, i.e., in a manner that makes this attack possible or even economically viable. In that case, it has a *vulnerability*.

Furthermore, following the constant increase in the available and affordable computing power, cryptographers, standards bodies, and regulators revisit algorithms and update them periodically to stay ahead of possible attackers. Staying ahead is usually achieved by either choosing methods that are entirely beyond the combined computational power of humankind or at least picking methods for which the cost of a possible forced attack is higher than the benefit.

1.3.2 Quantum computing

Quantum computers are based on different physical principles than traditional semiconductor-based electronics. So they can (on a small scale for now) solve some computational problems incomparably faster than conventional computers. At some point, quantum computers are expected to have solved a problem for which there is not enough traditional computational power in the world – a moment called *quantum supremacy*.

Although not yet ready for prime time, this technology will change the landscape significantly. Specifically, many methods that rely on factorization will no longer be strong enough for reasonable use.

For example, it is computationally easy to multiply two large prime numbers, but it is hard to find them knowing just their product – with deterministic computers. Conversely, quantum computers will quickly accomplish this task once they grow big.

Note that while quantum computing will render some cryptographic algorithms useless, not all algorithms will share this fate. In fact, the majority of algorithms that are in active use in payments are considered quantum-secure.

---

[1] Except for the one-time pad algorithm, which relies on a shared mutual random sequence of bits and is not used in practical applications

1.3.3 Basics terms and definitions

Cryptographic protocols speak of message exchange between sender and receiver. The unencrypted message is called *plaintext*, and the encrypted message is called *ciphertext*. Making message contents obscure to third parties is called *encryption* – it turns plaintext into ciphertext. The reverse process is *decryption*; it turns ciphertext into plaintext.

However, the simple act of obscuring a message's contents is not enough to keep it safe from an eavesdropper. The eavesdropper must also not possess the means to decrypt the message independently.

In modern cryptography, all algorithms are published in great detail for experts to analyze for deficiencies. This way, users can be confident that all algorithms do not have vulnerabilities. It also helps algorithm adoption by allowing multiple independent implementations. It also means that knowledge of the algorithm itself is not enough to keep the message secret. So, besides the message itself, any such algorithm must receive an additional parameter to encrypt or decrypt the message.

Such a parameter is called a *key*. The range of possible keys is called a *keyspace*. As mentioned above, no algorithm in the field is impossible to break. However, a well-designed algorithm will only allow brute-force attacks against itself, so the larger the keyspace, the stronger the algorithm is.

If an algorithm uses keys of 64-bit length, in theory, there are 2^{64} possible values of these keys, which would be the size of the keyspace. However, some algorithms do not utilize all bits in their keys. For instance, DES (see *Section 1.4.1 DES (DEA)*) uses one bit in each byte of the key value to check parity (see *A Bits and Digits* for details on parity bits), making its actual keyspace significantly smaller: for each of the eight bytes, only 7 bits are used, reducing the keyspace to 2^{56}

The standard notation for encryption and decryption is as follows: P denotes the plaintext message and C the corresponding ciphertext. The encryption function is E, while the decryption function is D.

The following notation is used to reflect that the encrypting or the decrypting function uses the key K:

$$E_K(P) = C$$

$$D_K(C) = P$$

For cryptography to work, these functions necessarily have the properties:

$$D_K(E_K(P)) \equiv P$$

$$E_K(D_K(C)) \equiv C$$

However, this notation implicitly assumes that the same key is used for both encryption and decryption. While true for the class of algorithms called *symmetric algorithms*, it is also possible to have a different key for encryption (K_1) and decryption (K_2). We therefore get

$$E_{K_1}(P) = C,$$

$$D_{K_2}(C) = P$$

and

$$D_{K_2}(E_{K_1}(P)) = P.$$

Cryptographic algorithms are also grouped into *block* and *stream algorithms* or *block ciphers* and *stream ciphers*, correspondingly.

A block cipher operates on a block of data of fixed size. For example, DES and Triple-DES algorithms operate on 64-bit data blocks, while the AES algorithm works on 128-bit data blocks. A stream cipher operates on a stream of bits. While this family of algorithms has its applications, it is not present in the payments space.

It is worth noting that, given a stream cipher, it is easy to construct a block cipher by applying the stream cipher to the block of data bit by bit. The opposite is also possible: for example, a block cipher can be invoked iteratively by feeding the output of a previous iteration as input into the next one. The result will be a sequence of bits which can then be XORed with the bitstream of the actual data (see also *Appendix A Bits and Digits* for more details on bit manipulations and *Section 1.8.1 Cipher block chaining* for details on iterative invocation of block ciphers).

1.3.4 Symmetric and asymmetric algorithms

If the keys for encryption and decryption differ, the algorithm is called *asymmetric algorithms*. This class of algorithms is often referred to as *public-key* cryptography, with the encryption key called the *public key* and the decryption key called the *private key*.

These names come from one of the first and more obvious applications of an asymmetric algorithm, which is securing communication one way, from the sender to the receiver only, for example, allowing anyone to send a private message to this receiver securely. In that scenario, the receiver generates a pair of keys and keeps the decryption key secret (hence the name "private") while publishing the encryption key for the world to see (hence the name "public").

Assuming that the algorithm is sufficiently strong and its keyspace is large enough, anyone will be able to encrypt their message with the public key and send it to the receiver, which, being the sole holder of the private key, is the only person able to decrypt the message. Furthermore, the encrypted message needs no protection from any interception since a third party that gets hold of it will not be able to read it without the private key.

With symmetric algorithms, the encryption and the decryption functions use the same key. Consequently, unlike the asymmetric case, it cannot be published and must be carefully shared with specific parties. Hence one of the terms used for the key of a symmetric algorithm is *secret*, and establishing a shared secret between multiple parties is not a simple task (see, for example, *Key Trust and Key Certificates Key Trust and Key Certificates* or *Section 5.2.2 Key exchange and management*).

It is possible to create an efficient hybrid system using both symmetric and asymmetric algorithms, keeping the benefits of both algorithm families without most of the drawbacks. For instance, the two communicating parties can use an asymmetric algorithm to establish a mutually shared session key, which will be symmetric. The TLS protocol (see *Section 4.1 Transport Layer Security (TLS)*) is the most widespread example of a hybrid system. Another example is the Elliptic-Curve Integrated Encryption Scheme (ECIES) (see *Section 1.6.3 Elliptic curve integrated encryption scheme (ECIES)*).

Public key cryptography is discussed in *Section 1.5 Public Key Cryptography*, and symmetric algorithms are further discussed in *Section 1.4 Symmetric Algorithms*.

1.4   Symmetric Algorithms

A symmetric algorithm is an algorithm that has identical encryption and decryption keys.

There are many symmetric algorithms in existence. However, in the field of payments, the industry tends to use only a couple of them, namely the Data Encryption Standard (*DES*) [1–3] and Advanced Encryption Standard (*AES*) [4,5]. Following the practice, we will only cover these two below.

Both DES and AES perform a reversible sequence of bit operations and substitutions to scramble the input and do not explicitly rely on an arithmetic computation.

The algorithmic information theory defines two properties of a secure cipher, *confusion* and *diffusion*.

Confusion means that a change of a single bit in the key affects the calculation of most or all of the bits in the ciphertext. The substitution steps of both algorithms are designed to provide high levels of confusion.

Diffusion means that a change of a single bit of the plaintext will change about half of the ciphertext bits and vice versa. Permutations used by both algorithms aim to provide diffusion.

1.4.1   DES (DEA)

The Data Encryption Standard was designed in the 1970s and was the first publicly available standard algorithm approved for government use [1–3].

The algorithm uses the initial 64-bit key as a starting point for a *key schedule* – a method to derive subkeys for use in the algorithm's substeps (called rounds).

While the overall length of the key is 8 bytes, the algorithm only uses 56 bits, and the remaining one bit per byte is used for parity.

The algorithm generates 48-bit subkeys by using a combination of bit shifts and a bit permutation table.

The input data passes a bit permutation first. The data is then split into half-blocks of 32 bits each.

On each iteration, the algorithm takes one-half of the input, expands it to 48 bits using a pre-defined table (mixing and duplicating input bits), then XORs it with the current subkey.

After the XOR operation, the bits are fed into a *substitution box* (*S-box*), a predefined table that maps 6-bit values into 4-bit outputs, thus reducing the 48-bit expanded value back to 32 bits.

Then, the value passes through a *permutation box* (*P-box*) which permutates the bits.

After this step, the two halves of the input are swapped, and in the next round, the former right half of the input data undergoes the steps above. See *Section* 1.1 for an illustration of this method, also called *Feistel's process* (see Figure 1.1).

Finally, when the entire cycle of 16 rounds is completed, the output undergoes another bit permutation, and the encrypted value is ready.

The algorithm has four known "weak" and 12 "semi-weak" keys. For instance, a sequence of 8 0xFE bytes is a weak key. If the DES key is generated

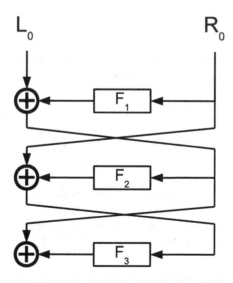

Figure 1.1: Feistel's process of the DES algorithm.

using a random number generator, the probability of obtaining such a key is very low. However, some implementations, such as the OpenSSL library (see *Appendix B.5 DES and Triple DES*), check their input values for the known weak and semi-weak keys.

The algorithm was already considered weak in the 1990s and today serves only as a building block together with various flavors of the Triple-DES mode of operation (see *Section 1.8.1 Padding and cipher block chaining*). For example, the first step of the CVV calculation still uses DES as the encryption algorithm (see *Section 3.2.1 CVV/CVC calculation and CVKs*).

As DES stands for "Data Encryption Standard," in some cases, a distinction is made between the standard and the algorithm it describes. In this case, the algorithm is referred to as the "Data Encryption Algorithm" or DEA.

1.4.2 AES

The Advanced Encryption Standard [4, 5] was established in 2001 after an open selection process that took into account input from independent researchers. The algorithm was selected from a shortlist of several candidates and later adopted by the US government as the replacement for DES.

The algorithm can work with 128-, 192- and 256-bit keys to encrypt a 128-bit input. Like DES, AES derives "round keys" from the input key, with the number of rounds depending on the key size. For brevity, the AES algorithms with different key lengths are sometimes referred to as *AES-128*, *AES-192*, and *AES-256*, correspondingly.

Each round key is 128 bits. At the beginning of the algorithm, a round key is first XORed with the input data. This step is called *AddRoundKey*.

Then, iterating through rounds, the algorithm performs the *SubBytes* step, where an S-box mechanism with carefully designed substitution tables is applied to the data bits.

After the substitution, the algorithm treats the data as a matrix and performs a *ShiftRows* operation (reshuffling rows so that elements of each column in the matrix intermingle) and a *MixColumns* step which applies a linear transformation to each column of the matrix. Finally, the result is XORed with the round key in another *AddRoundKey* invocation.

After the substitution, the algorithm treats the data as a matrix and performs a *ShiftRows* operation (reshuffling rows so that elements of each column in the matrix intermingle) and a *MixColumns* step which applies a linear transformation to each column of the matrix. Finally, the result is XORed with the round key in another *AddRoundKey* invocation.

As with DES, AES performs well on different hardware. It allows further optimization for speed with lookup tables for some of the steps. Built-in AES instructions are also available in many processors (e.g., x86 architecture).

1.5 Public Key Cryptography

The term public key cryptography refers to a family of asymmetric cryptographic protocols. The vast majority rely on certain functions' algebraic properties and computational complexity over finite fields.

Public key cryptography is very convenient from the point of view of key management. Public key algorithms make it easy to provide keys for one-way communication or establish a shared secret key. However, practically, symmetric algorithms which rely on bit permutations have several significant advantages over the public-key algorithms: they are easy to implement in hardware, they are much faster to compute and require shorter key lengths for the same cryptographic strength, and, finally, many of symmetric algorithms are quantum-safe.

For the first two reasons, public key cryptography is often used to establish a mutual key (see *Section 1.5.2 Diffie-Hellman key exchange (DHE)*), use it to exchange a symmetric session key, and then stay with the symmetric algorithm for the duration of the session.

A group of standards exists in public key cryptography under *Public Key Cryptography Standards (PKCS)*. These are typically referred to under a number. For example, PKCS #1 covers the RSA cryptography standard.

1.5.1 RSA

Perhaps the oldest encryption algorithm in this field is RSA [6], which relies on the computational difficulty of number factorization. According to the algorithm, a part of each key is a large product of two large prime numbers. Breaking the encryption requires finding a root of the ciphertext over the ring of integers modulo the large number, which is computationally easy only if the two primes become known.

The RSA algorithm supports two modes: encryption and signature.

Under the encryption scenario, the receiver publishes the encryption key and keeps the decryption key secret. The sender can then use the public key to encrypt the message, and only the receiver can decrypt it.

Under the signature scenario, the role of the keys is converse. The signing party calculates the message hash and then encrypts it using their private key. Any party with the public key can use it to decrypt the signature and compare it to the independently calculated message hash value.

Both the public and the private key are a pair of numbers. The algorithm uses arithmetics for encryption, which assumes a certain message length (size of the number), and is, therefore, a block cipher.

The public key for the algorithm is a pair of two numbers, a product of two primes p and q, called the *modulus* and denoted as n, and a number e that is coprime with the least common multiple of $p-1$ and $q-1$, λ. In practice, to simplify computations, e is usually chosen to be either 3 or $2^{2^4} + 1 = 65537$

(both prime numbers) and pre-defined for the entire protocol. The number e is also called the *public exponent*.

The private key is the pair of two numbers, n and d, where the latter is a modular multiplicative inverse of e modulo λ. The actual calculation is more straightforward than it looks; see *Appendix B.2 RSA* for an example with small numbers. The number d is also called the *private exponent*.

It turns out[2] that M to the power of ed is always equal to M modulo n.

Hence, the algorithm does the following to encrypt and decrypt the data.

To encrypt the message M, the sender raises it to the power of e modulo n. To decrypt the message, the recipient raises the encrypted message to the power of d modulo n.

$$C \equiv M^e \ mod \ n$$

$$M \equiv C^d \ mod \ n$$

Note that the length of the output of the encryption is equal to the length of the modulus, and this algorithm is a form of a block cipher.

Unfortunately, the computational complexity on which this elegant algorithm relies is only valid for deterministic computers. There are ways to break the encryption using a quantum computer quickly. However, no quantum computer today has enough qubits to get anywhere close to the key complexity used in the field.

The RSA cryptography standard is covered by PKCS #1 with the latest version published as RFC 8017 [8].

An example of the RSA algorithm can be found at *Appendix B.2 RSA*.

1.5.2 *Diffie-Hellman key exchange (DHE)*

The Diffie-Hellman key exchange algorithm is not a method to encrypt or sign data but rather an algorithm for public key exchange – that is, an algorithm which allows the setup of a secret key between the sender and the receiver over an unprotected public channel.

In its original form [9], the algorithm relies on the abovementioned fact that it is easy to calculate an exponent in a finite field but computationally hard to calculate a discrete logarithm. The protocol works as follows:

1. The sender and the receiver publicly agree on a prime number p and a primitive root g modulo p.

2. The sender chooses a secret integer, a, and calculates the value of A: $A \equiv g^a \ mod \ p$.

---

[2]This follows from Fermat's little theorem. A proof can be found, for example, on the Wikipedia page for the RSA cryptosystem [7].

3. *A* is then sent to the receiver.

4. The receiver chooses a secret integer, *b*, and calculates the value of *B*:
   $B \equiv g^b \bmod p$.

5. *B* is then transmitted to the sender.

6. The sender calculates $A^b \bmod p$, and the receiver calculates $B^a \bmod p$.

7. After completing these steps, they possess the same secret value, $A^b \equiv (g^a)^b \equiv B^a \equiv g^{b^a} \equiv g^{ab} \bmod p$, the shared secret key.

The protocol is also called *finite field Diffie-Hellman* to distinguish it from the elliptic-curve Diffie-Hellman (see *Section 1.6.2 Elliptic curve Diffie-Hellman (ECDH)*).

The Diffie-Hellman Key Agreement Standard is covered in PKCS #3 and RFC 2631 [10].

For a specific example, see *Appendix B.3 Diffie-Hellman Key Exchange*.

1.5.3 Shamir's Secret Sharing (SSS)

The Diffie-Hellman key exchange facilitates the exchange of a key between two parties. Shamir's secret sharing algorithm is an interesting generalization of this method, which is sometimes acceptable in payments.

The algorithm addresses the following problem: share parts of a secret across m custodians in a manner where any *k* of them can assemble and recover the secret, but for $k - 1$ or fewer custodians, recovery of the secret is as hard as for 0 custodians.

The algorithm is based on the following principle: given a polynomial of order $k - 1$, its coefficients can be recovered if *k* distinct points on the polynomial graph are known.

Shamir's method is as follows: to create a *k–of–m* secret sharing scheme, let the secret *S* be the constant term of a polynomial of order $k - 1$, and select the rest of its coefficients at random. If $P(x)$ is the resulting polynomial, calculate *m* points of it of the form $\langle 1, P(1) \rangle$, $\langle 2, P(2) \rangle$, and so on, and distribute the values to the custodians.

If the arithmetics are performed over a finite field, the resulting scheme will work as required (but will not provide the necessary secrecy otherwise). The polynomial's coefficients, including the sought constant term, can be reconstructed from any *k* points, while having less than *k* points make this task computationally difficult.

An example can be found in *Appendix B.4 Shamir's Secret Sharing*.

1.6 Elliptic-Curve Cryptography (ECC)

1.6.1 Background

The RSA algorithm relies on the fact that for $C \equiv M^e \bmod n$, it is hard to find the number d such that $C^d \equiv M \bmod n$ given C, M, and e. Likewise, the Diffie-Helman key exchange scheme relies on the fact that, given A, g, and p, it is hard to find a such that $A \equiv g^a \bmod p$. This step is equivalent to the calculation of the discrete logarithm. While some algorithms exist that speed up this calculation, it is still prohibitively difficult with a deterministic computer for keys of 2048 bits and longer.

This family of algorithms has the drawback of requiring CPU-heavy calculations on very large numbers. In an attempt to reduce the required computing power for the involved parties while retaining the computational difficulty, researchers came up with a method that relies on more advanced mathematical principles, called *elliptic-curve cryptography (ECC)*.

The full math behind this family of algorithms is beyond the scope of this book, but a basic understanding is nevertheless necessary.

An *elliptic curve* is a set of points $\langle x, y \rangle$ satisfying the condition $y^2 = x^3 + ax + b$. It would be a line similar to those found in Figure 1.2 on the real plane.

It is possible to define an addition operation on the points of an elliptic curve.

If an elliptic curve is taken on the projective plane (i.e., with the additional infinity point, $\mathfrak{O}$), the point addition between two points on the curve can be defined geometrically: to add two points on the curve, P and Q, draw the line

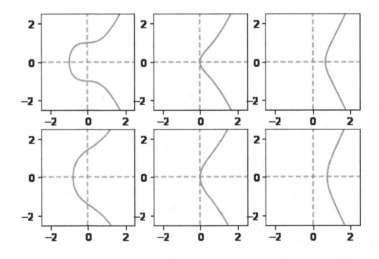

Figure 1.2: Examples of elliptic curves.

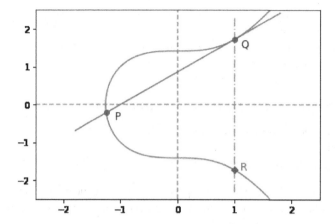

Figure 1.3: Elliptic curves point addition.

through them, find a third point where it intersects the curve and take its opposite relative to the X-axis, R, to be $R = P \cdot Q$ (see Figure 1.3)[3].

With the addition of the infinity point, this operation follows the group law over the curve. Furthermore, this algebraic structure remains valid over real numbers and a finite field. The latter can either be a field of remainders modulo a prime number (Z_p) or a field of polynomials with binary coefficients ($GF(2^n)$).

In other words, given an elliptic curve, a particular point on the curve, G, and an integer number M, we can define multiplication by an integer scalar: using point addition, add G to itself M times, and obtain the value of $C = M \cdot G$.

It turns out that if the elliptic curve has certain properties, it is computationally easy to calculate C given M and G but computationally hard to find M given C and G. This issue is also called the problem of a discrete logarithm on an elliptic curve and this problem is computationally much harder than the simple discrete logarithm.

To give an estimate [11], the computational power required to break a 2048-bit RSA key is roughly equivalent to the power required to break a 168-bit ECC key. Besides requiring shorter keys, the ECC-based operations of encryption, decryption, and key generation all outperform RSA operations of equivalent cryptographic strength. Unfortunately, the ECC is also more vulnerable to quantum algorithms.

Not every elliptic curve, field, or point G yield a computationally hard discrete logarithm. In a manner somewhat similar to how public exponents for RSA are usually chosen from only a few numbers, standard lists of cryptographically

---

[3]For special cases such as point doubling a tangent line is used, and the infinity point is also a member of the group.

strong elliptic curves are available, for example, from the National Institute of Standards and Technology [12].

The complete set of parameters of an elliptic curve, including the base point *G*, is called *domain parameters*.

1.6.2 Elliptic curve Diffie-Hellman (ECDH)

A version of the Diffie-Hellman key establishment protocol exists with elliptic curves [13].

The protocol works as follows:

1. The sender and the receiver publicly agree on domain parameters, i.e., select an elliptic curve. The set of domain parameters would include the elliptic curve base point, *G*.

2. The sender randomly selects an integer, d_A, which is the sender's private key. The sender then publishes the point $Q_A = d_A \cdot G$, which is the sender's public key.

3. The receiver randomly selects an integer, d_B. The receiver then publishes $Q_B = d_B \cdot G$.

4. The sender computes $K = d_A \cdot Q_B = (d_A d_B) \cdot G$.

5. The receiver computes $K = d_B \cdot Q_A = (d_A d_B) \cdot G$.

6. Both parties can now use the first coordinate of K as the mutually shared secret key.

1.6.3 Elliptic curve integrated encryption scheme (ECIES)

An *integrated encryption scheme* is an encryption scheme that utilizes both asymmetric and symmetric algorithms. The asymmetric algorithm establishes a mutually shared secret key for the symmetric algorithm, which is then used to encrypt the data.

The ECIES picks up where ECDH has left off. Once the mutual secret, based on elliptic-curve cryptography, has been established, both the sender and the receiver use a particular *key derivation function* (*KDF*) to generate a pair of keys for encryption and for *message authentication code* (*MAC*), based on the first coordinate of the curve point that they have recovered. See also *Section 1.9 Message Authentication Codes* for details on MACs.

Each message is then encrypted and signed with two different keys, both identical since they were derived from the same initial value.

1.7 Hash Functions

A *hash function* is a function that transforms a variable-length input (called the *pre-image*, following the mathematical terminology for functions) into a fixed-length output (the *hash*). Unlike the cryptographic algorithms mentioned above, whose primary goal is to preserve confidentiality, hash functions primarily help ensure message integrity. As with other algorithms, there is no "unbreakable" hash function, but "breaking" has a different meaning in this domain.

Breaking a hash function means that an attacker was able to generate or modify a pre-image in a manner that will yield the same value of the hash. The formal term for this is *collision*, and a good hash function is *collision-free*, i.e., it is computationally hard to generate such two pre-images from a given hash value. This property of hash functions is one of the cornerstones of cryptocurrencies (see also *Section 2.2.4 Cryptocurrencies*).

An obvious application for hash functions is to ensure the integrity of files. For example, a vendor can distribute software updates through various channels such as mirror download sites, even if some cannot be fully trusted. The vendor can also publish a list of hash values for each update file it distributes. Its customers can then download the files from the most convenient source, calculate the hash value independently for each file and compare the result to the authoritative list by the vendor. If the hash function is sufficiently strong, a potential attacker will not be able to inject malware into the software updates and have it retain the same hash value.

Hash functions can also provide message authentication in addition to message integrity. The sender can append a secret value (also called *salt* or *secret*) to the message. The sender and the receiver both know the value, but the sender does not transmit it alongside the message.

Adding salt is also a countermeasure against dictionary attacks: for example, it is common to store passwords after a transformation by some hash function. If the attackers gain access to hashes, they will not be able to reverse the hash and restore the passwords. However, the attacker can prepare a dictionary of common passwords and their hash values, and compare only the hashes, thus identifying known passwords. Adding salt (which can be made quite big) will increase the dictionary size to non-feasible dimensions.

The receiver has all the necessary information to validate message integrity and ensure it originated from the sender, as only the sender knows the secret value. An attacker wishing to pose as the sender or modify the message will have to break the hash, which is computationally hard.

When used in such a manner, a message hash (with some extra tweaks) is sometimes called a *message authentication code* (*MAC*). It is also possible to use block ciphers to compute message authentication codes by chaining them (one such method is described in *Section 1.8.1 Padding and cipher block chaining*).

Message authentication codes are described in more detail in *Section 1.9 Message Authentication Codes*. It is worth noting that the mentioned approach (appending a secret to the hash and then using it to ensure message authenticity) with some hash functions is vulnerable to attacks where the attacker cannot change the original message but can extend it.

Some of the widely used hash functions are *MD5* [14] and *SHA-1* [15]. The former, "Message Digest 5," generates 16-byte hash values, while the latter, "Secure Hash Algorithm 1," generates 20-byte values. Both are cryptographically broken, and effective attacks were demonstrated against them. However, they remain widely used.

The next generation of hash functions is the *Secure Hash Algorithm 2* [15] family, consisting of six hash functions with different hash sizes. The hashes are *SHA-224, SHA-256, SHA-384, SHA-512, SHA-512/224,* and *SHA-512/256*. The SHA-224 and SHA-384 are both a version of SHA-256 and SHA-512 with a slight difference in initialization and the output value truncated. SHA-512/224 and SHA 512/256 are truncated versions of SHA-512 with minor initialization differences.

A newer standard, *SHA-3* or *Secure Hash Algorithm 3* [16], also exists. However, since SHA-2 is considered to have adequate security, SHA-3 hashes have a much smaller footprint in the field.

The MD5, SHA-1, and SHA-2 hash functions share a common architecture, the *Merkle-Damgård construction*. With it, the input value is padded in a manner that also encodes its length. Then, internal state variables are initialized, and for each block of input data, a variety of bitwise and arithmetical operations are applied to the state variables. At the end of the input, the state is output as the hash value.

1.8 Combining Algorithms

The algorithms mentioned above are rarely used on their own. Instead, these algorithms should be considered building blocks for more elaborate protocols and methods.

1.8.1 Padding and cipher block chaining

1.8.1.1 Padding

As mentioned above, block ciphers operate on blocks of fixed-length data. Such an algorithm is not universally applicable as-is since data length in various scenarios can differ.

In case when the data is shorter than the block length, the solution is to pad the input data to the length of the block. Padding is used, for example, with card PIN values which rarely are as long as 6 digits, whereas even the smaller DES/TDES block is 8 bytes and can contain at least 16 decimal digits (see also *Section 3.4.3.1 PIN block format 2 and offline plaintext validation, Section 3.4.3.4 PIN block formats 0, 1, 3, and 4*).

Multiple approaches for padding exist [17]. The value can be padded to the block size multiple with zero bits (*ISO 9797 padding method 1*) or a single 1 bit and then zeros until full block size (*ISO 9797 padding method 2*). Data length can be put at the beginning of the padded data, followed by the data itself, followed by enough zero bits to fill the block size multiple (*ISO 9797 padding method 3*).

1.8.1.2 Optimal asymmetric encryption padding (OAEP)

A more advanced method for padding, typically used with asymmetric algorithms, is the *optimal asymmetric encryption padding (OAEP)* [8].

The method relies on a cryptographic primitive called the *mask generation function (MGF)*. A mask generation function is a hash function that can produce outputs of an arbitrary length. The input parameter of the function will fully determine its entire output. As part of the OAEP method, one such function, MGF1, was also defined.

MGF1 is quite simple: given a hash function H and a seed S, generate a string of bits $H(S \parallel C)$, where C is a four-byte counter running from 0. The process should continue until the desired number of output bytes is generated.

The padding itself relies on the MGF function. A variant of SHA hash is most frequently used; in the notion of OAEP-xxxx, the suffix indicates the specific SHA function. For example, for OAEP-256 it is SHA-256.

In the following, *hLen* is the length of the output of the chosen hash function (for OAEP-256 it will be 256 bits), and k is the desired length of the output.

An optional label, L, may be attached to the message M.

As part of the algorithm (see also Figure 1.4):

1. L is hashed with H to obtain $L_H = H(L)$. If L is empty, a default value is used instead.

2. M is padded to the value of $k - hLen - 1$, or in other words, the desired length minus one byte and a length of one hash output. The padding format is as follows: L_H, followed by the required number of zeroes, followed by the fixed value of 0x01, followed by the message M. The outcome is the data block D: $D = L_H \parallel 0..0 \parallel 0x01 \parallel M$.

3. A random seed S is generated. Its length must be *hLen*.

4. The seed S is used to generate a mask, X_d, for the data block. Its length is equal to the size of D.

5. The mask is XORed with the data block: $D' = X_d \oplus D$. At this point, we have a padded message, XORed with a pseudorandom bit sequence. Since

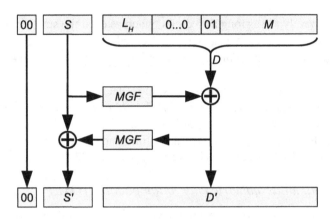

Figure 1.4: OAEP padding.

the recipient does not know the seed S, they have no way to recover the data unless we find a way to transmit the seed securely. The seed is transmitted in the following steps.

6. The result of step 5, D', is used as a seed for another mask of length $hLen$, X_S.

7. The mask, X_S, is XORed with the seed S to obtain $S' = S \oplus X_S$.

8. The full padded message consists of a fixed value of 0x00, then S', then D'.

To recover the message, the recipient needs to perform the following steps:

1. Split the S' and the D' from the input.

2. Use D' as the seed for a mask X_S.

3. Recover S via $S = X_S \oplus S'$.

4. Use S as the seed for a mask X_D.

5. Recover D via $D = X_D \oplus D'$.

6. Validate L_H and process the message by skipping the zero bytes after L_H and the 0x01 sentinel byte before the payload.

An example of OAEP can be found in *Appendix B.7 OAEP*.

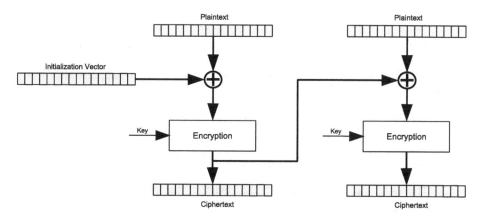

Figure 1.5: CBC encryption.

1.8.1.3 Electronic code book (ECB) and cipher block chaining (CBC)

When the data to be encrypted is longer than the block size, the evident approach is to pad the data to a length that divides by block size, then encrypt each block separately.

This method is called the *electronic code book* (*ECB*) mode. It is simple to comprehend and implement, but it also has a flaw: identical data blocks will be encrypted into identical ciphertext blocks, no matter where they are or when they occurred over the communication session. Since real-life communication protocols tend to have similar beginnings and endings for messages, and data often comes with repeating patterns, an attacker can collect a code book of known or repeating encrypted segments and then use it to analyze the encrypted messages or simplify the task of breaking the encryption.

Furthermore, the ECB approach does not preserve integrity. While it is impossible to modify a single bit or a single byte in a single block, given a code book, it is easy to replace a block with another block, tampering with the encrypted message.

These vulnerabilities can be mitigated by changing the keys frequently and adding a MAC, but a more elegant solution exists.

This solution is *chaining*, and its underlying principle is to feed the encrypted result of the previous block into the next one. This mode of operation of block ciphers is called *cipher block chaining* (*CBC*), and its flow for encryption is as follows (see also Figure 1.5):

1. The data is padded and split into blocks, P_i.

2. Block P_i for $i > 1$ is XORed with the result of the previous iteration, C_{i-1}.

3. The outcome is encrypted using the key K: $C_i = E_K(P_i \oplus C_{i-1})$.

4. The outcome is sent to the output and stored for the next iteration.

For decryption, the flow is similar, except that the XOR happens after the decryption (see also Figure 1.6):

1. The enciphered data already has the correct padding, so it is only split into blocks, C_i.

2. Block C_i is decrypted using the key K.

3. The outcome is XORed with the result of the previous iteration: $P_i = D_K(C_{i-1}) \oplus P_{i-1}$.

4. The outcome is sent to the output and stored for the next iteration.

The two algorithms above describe all steps except for the first one. There is no result of the previous iteration for the first data block with which it can be XORed prior to encryption and, conversely, after the decryption. It is possible to use zero values as that initial XOR mask since the bitwise operation will not affect the value. However, with this approach, two identical plaintext messages will result in two identical ciphertexts, and two similar plaintext messages will yield identical ciphertexts until the first difference.

The first data block is XORed with a random data block to address that. Such a block is called the *initialization vector* (*IV*), and it can be sent in the clear alongside the ciphertext without weakening the protocol.

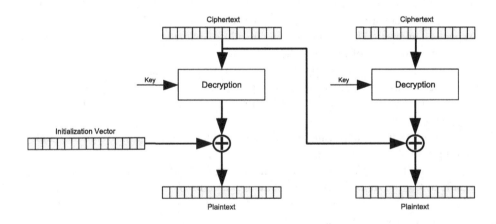

Figure 1.6: CBC decryption.

1.8.2 Combined ciphers

The methods mentioned in *Section 1.8.1 Padding and cipher block chaining* allow applying a block cipher to data of bigger size than a single block, allowing the application of a particular block cipher to data of arbitrary length.

However, recombining block ciphers is another way to increase their cryptographic strength. A simple way to strengthen the encryption of a block cipher without reengineering its internals is by performing it consequently, several times, with different keys. In payments, this was applied to the DES algorithm as the original DES encryption became obsolete due to the rapid growth of computational power [18].

It is possible to double or triple the key length of an algorithm by defining the following encryption function:

$$E'(P) = E_{K_1}(D_{K_2}(E_{K_3}(P)))$$

$$D'(C) = D_{K_1}(E_{K_2}(D_{K_3}(C)))$$

This method of applying block ciphers is called the *encrypt-decrypt-encrypt* (*EDE*) mode [19].

Here, all three values K_1, K_2, and K_3 can differ, tripling the effective key length. With DES, the keyspace grows from 2^{56} to 2^{168} – a significant improvement.

It is possible to set K_1 equal to K_3. In that case, the key length will be double compared to the original algorithm; with DES, this means going from a keyspace of 2^{56} to 2^{112}.

Finally, and by design, such a combined algorithm is backward compatible. If the value of $K_1 = K_2 = K_3$, the result is identical to $E_{K_1}(P)$. Modern secure devices, especially those used in payments, can detect and block such attempts for the DES algorithm.

The enhanced DES algorithm in the EDE mode with at least two keys is called *Triple DES*, denoted as *3DES*, *TDES*, or *TDEA*.

1.9 Message Authentication Codes

MACs or *message authentication codes* are a mechanism to authenticate the message sender. Such authentication requires establishing a shared secret key between the sender and the receiver. Message authentication code is sometimes called *message integrity code* (*MICs*), *message digest*, or simply *tag*.

There are at least two possibilities to compute a MAC: with a hash function or a block cipher.

The basic implementations are as follows.

With the hash function approach, the sender appends the secret key to the message and hashes the result. The sender then transmits the message and the hash to the receiver. The receiver, knowing the secret, calculates the hash independently and validates it.

With the block cipher approach, the sender uses the secret key for a cipher block chaining message encryption with a zero initialization vector. The sender then transmits the message and the result of the last iteration as the MAC. The overall is unsurprisingly called *cipher block chaining message authentication code* (*CBC-MAC*).

This approach is valid for messages of fixed length or such where the length is sent in the message header (or in another location at the beginning of the transmission). If the length varies and is not sent at the beginning of the message, an attack called *length-extension* can be used to add more data to the message[4].

Among the well-known hash algorithms, MD5, SHA-1, and SHA-2 are susceptible to this type of attack, while SHA-3, SHA-384, and SHA-512/256 are not [21].

The ISO/IEC 9797 standard specifies MAC types and various algorithms used to calculate them [17, 22, 23].

Further developments of the idea exist which fix that vulnerability. For CBC-based MACs, there is, for example, the *ECBC-MAC* algorithm, also known as *encrypt-last-block*, where after the final iteration of the CBC with the first secret key, it is encrypted once with a second secret key.

A method to calculate message authentication codes using polynomials over a finite field is called *Galois message authentication code* (*GMAC*) and is briefly described in *1.9.6 Galois/Counter Mode*.

1.9.1 CMAC

Another option for block cipher-based MACs suitable for variable-length messages is an algorithm called *One-Key MAC* (*OMAC1*), also referred to as *CMAC*: with this algorithm, the last (padded) chunk of the plaintext is XORed with a key derived from the pre-shared secret (see Figure 1.7).

Assume that K is the original key and that M is the message. The algorithm begins by deriving keys K_1 and K_2:

1. A block of zeroes is encrypted with K to obtain K_0: $K_0 = E(0)$.

2. If the most significant bit of K_0 is 0, $K_1 = K_0 \ll 1$. Otherwise, $K_1 = K_0 \ll 1 \oplus C$, where C is a well-known constant that only depends on the block size.

3. If the most significant bit of K_1 is 0, $K_2 = K_1 \ll 1$. Otherwise, $K_2 = K_1 \ll 1 \oplus C$, where C is the same constant as the previous step.

---

[4]For example, in 2009 researchers Thai Duong and Juliano Rizzo used the attack to compromise Flickr [20].

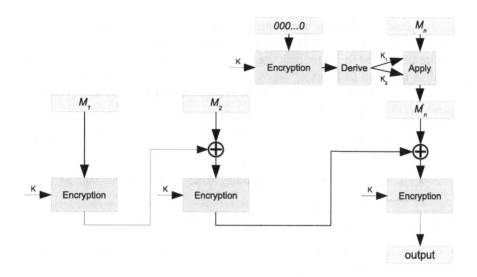

Figure 1.7: OMAC1 calculation.

The algorithm then uses one of the keys to adjust the input value. If M is divided into chunks $M_1 \ldots M_n$, the last chunk may or may not be of the full size of the encryption algorithm input block.

If the size of M_n is equal to that of the input block, it is XOR'ed with K_1. Otherwise, it is padded with a single set bit and then with zero bits up to the full length of the input block (ISO 9797 padding method 2). The result is XOR'ed with K_2 to obtain M_n', the new trailing chunk of the message M.

The algorithm continues with CBC encryption of the updated M with an IV of 0. The output of the last iteration is the CMAC value for M.

An example calculation of a CMAC can be found in *B.9 HMAC and CMAC*.

1.9.2 HMAC

For hash-based MACs, there is an algorithm called *hash message authentication code (HMAC)* [24]. The HMAC works with any hash function and any block size of the hash function.

The HMAC takes a secret key, K, and the message M as the input.

To calculate the HMAC, the sender first makes sure the secret has the same size as the hash function internal block. If it is longer than the block size, the secret is hashed with the hash function; if it is shorter than the block size, it is right-padded with zero.

In other words, if the length of K is greater than the hash function's H internal block size, $K' = H(K)$ is used instead of K.

Two padding values are used with the HMAC algorithm, the inner (*ipad*) and the outer (*opad*) paddings. The inner padding is the value of 0x36, repeated to the size of K', and the outer padding is the value of 0x5c, repeated to the same length as the inner padding.

The output is calculated according to the formula: $HMAC(K,M) = H((K' \oplus opad) \| H(K' \oplus ipad) \| M))$:

1. The secret K is adjusted to the block size by either padding or hashing, yielding K'.

2. K' is XORed with the inner padding (0x36), and the message M is appended to it.

3. The result is hashed using H to obtain the intermediate value V_1.

4. K' is XORed with the outer padding (0x5c), and the intermediate value of V_1 is appended to it.

5. The result is hashed to obtain the HMAC.

An example calculation of an HMAC can be found in *Appendix B.9 HMAC and CMAC*.

1.9.3 DSS (DSA)

NIST published the *Digital Signature Standard* (*DSS*) in 1994 [25]. Similarly to DES, the algorithm is sometimes referred to as Digital Signature Algorithm (DSA) to distinguish it from the standard.

The DSS relies on a discrete logarithm's computational difficulty and a few arithmetics principles over a finite field.

If p is prime and g is appropriately chosen, it is easy to calculate $y \equiv g^x \bmod p$ for a number x, but hard to find x given g, y, and p. Given two numbers, x and k, with $y \equiv g^x \bmod p$ and $z \equiv g^k \bmod p$, the recipient can compute the g to the power of any linear combination of x and k with only y and z:

$$g^{ax+bk} = g^{xa} \cdot g^{kb} = (g^x)^a \cdot (g^k)^b = y^a \cdot z^b$$

In a simplified manner, the DSS uses that fact to sign a message as follows: If m is a number that we want to sign using two secrets, x and k, we can prove that we have access to these secrets by crafting a linear combination of them, so that $m = ax + bk$, and then the recipient can calculate g^m with g and m, and g^{ax+bk} with g^x and g^k, without knowing the secrets, if the sender provides some information on a and b.

Since the signature algorithm must work on messages of an arbitrary length, the standard prescribes first applying a hash function to the message. In the initial version, the hash function was SHA-1. In the later revisions of the standard, stronger hash functions are allowed, and only several leading bytes of their output are taken as m.

The DSS works as follows. To prepare the keys:

1. Prime p is chosen, and q is a prime divisor of $p - 1$.

2. $g = h^{\frac{p-1}{q}}$, where $1 < h < p - 1$ such that $h^{\frac{p-1}{q}} \bmod p > 1$. The values p, q, and g are the domain parameters of the algorithm and can be shared among many parties.

3. x is a randomly chosen number, the private key, $0 < x < q$.

4. Compute $y \equiv g^x \bmod p$. y is the public key.

To sign the message M:

1. Compute $m = H(M)$ where H is the SHA-1 hash function.

2. Choose a random number k such that $0 < k < q$. k is kept secret and is different for each signature.

3. Set $r = (g^k \bmod p) \bmod q$.

4. Set $s = k^{-1}(m + xr) \bmod q$.

The pair of values r and s is the signature. Note that $m \equiv ks - xr \ (mod\ q)$, a linear combination of k and x. k^{-1} is such that $k^{-1} \cdot k \equiv 1 \ mod\ q$.

To verify the signature, the recipient has g, p, q, y, r, and s, as well as the message M.

1. Compute $m = H(M)$ using the SHA-1 algorithm.

2. Compute $w = s^{-1} \ mod\ q$. Note that $w = (m + xr)^{-1} k \ mod\ q$, but the recipient does not know x and k.

3. Compute $u_1 = mw \ mod\ q$. Here, $u_1 = (m + xr)^{-1} km \ mod\ q$.

4. Compute $u_2 = rw \ mod\ q$. Here, $u_2 = (m + xr)^{-1} kr \ mod\ q$.

5. Compute $v = ((g^{u_1})(y^{u_2}) \ mod\ p) \ mod\ q$. If $v = r$, the signature is valid.

To understand why it works consider the expression of

$$u_1 + xu_2 = (m + xr)^{-1}km + (m + xr)^{-1}krx = k(m + xr)^{-1}(m + rx) = k$$

Due to the choice of p and q and some properties of finite fields, we can actually substitute the values above and obtain:

$$g^{u_1} y^{u_2} \ mod\ p \equiv g^{u_1} g^{xu_2} \ mod\ p \equiv g^{u_1 + xu_2} \ mod\ p$$

which, if the values of s and r correspond to m, yield $gk \equiv r \ mod\ p$.

An example calculation of DSS can be found in *Appendix B.8 DSS (DSA)*.

1.9.4 ECDSA

The *elliptic-curve digital signature algorithm (ECDSA)* uses very similar principles as the DSS (see *Section 1.9.3 DSS (DSA)*) but relies on scalar multiplication of points on an elliptic curve instead of raising to power over a finite field. Refer to *Section 1.6 Elliptic-Curve Cryptography (ECC)* to better understand the underlying principles of point addition on a curve.

For the ECDSA, the idea is the same as with DSS: the first leading bytes of the message hash, m, are represented as a linear combination of two points on the curve. The sender knows the generating scalars for these points and can efficiently compute them. The recipient can validate that the computation matches m without knowing the secret values.

The key generation for ECDSA works as follows:

1. Pick an elliptic curve.

2. Find a point G on the curve such that $p \cdot G = \mho$, where p is a prime number.

3. Randomly select the private key, d_A, such that $0 < d_A < p$, and compute the public key, $Q_A = d_A \cdot G$.

To sign the message M:

1. Compute $H(M)$, message hash value, and take a pre-defined number of leading bits as m.

2. Choose a random number k such that $0 < k < p$. The number must be unique for each message.

3. Calculate $\langle x_1, y_1 \rangle = k \cdot G$.

4. Let $r = x_1 \bmod p$.

5. Let $s = k^{-1}(m + rd_A) \bmod p$. Note that $m \equiv ks - rd_A \bmod p$.

6. If r or s is zero, repeat from step 2.

7. The signature is the pair (r, s).

To verify the signature:

1. Calculate m based on the message.

2. Let $u_1 = ms^{-1} \bmod p$. Note that u_1 equals $mk(m + rd_A)^{-1} \bmod p$.

3. Let $u_2 = rs^{-1} \bmod p$. Note that u_2 equals $x_1 k(m + rd_A)^{-1} \bmod p$.

4. Calculate the curve point $u - 1 \cdot G + u_2 \cdot Q_A$. Its first coordinate must be equal to $r \bmod p$.

This method works since

$$u_1 \cdot G + u_2 \cdot Q_A = u_1 \cdot G + u_2 d_A \cdot G = (u_1 + u_2 d_A) \cdot G =$$
$$= (mk(m + rd_A)^{-1} + x_1 k d_A (m + rd_A)^{-1}) \cdot G =$$
$$= k(m + x_1 d_A)(m + rd_A)^{-1} \cdot G$$

Since $p \cdot G = \mathfrak{O}$, the scalar can be taken modulo p, and we obtain

$$k(m + x_1 d_A)(m + rd_A)^{-1} \cdot G = k \cdot G = \langle x_1, y_1 \rangle$$

1.9.5 Authenticated encryption

There are many various possible attacks on a cryptographic system. One of them is the *chosen-ciphertext attack*, when the attacker creates ciphertext messages and submits them to a decrypting mechanism to analyze the results and learn something about the key used.

A method for data encryption such as listed in *1.4 Symmetric Algorithms* would be vulnerable to this type of attack. In order to counter this vulnerability, encryption is augmented with message authentication. This hybrid model is called *authenticated encryption (AE)*.

Multiple methods exist to implement authenticated encryption, including algorithms explicitly designed to perform both encryption and authentication. However, combining two well-known algorithms (encryption and MAC) is much more prevalent in the field.

There are three major approaches to the authenticated encryption algorithm. These are *Encrypt-then-Mac (EtM)*, *Encrypt-and-Mac (E&M)*, and *Mac-then-Encrypt (MtE)*.

Like the names imply, with EtM, two keys are used to encrypt the ciphertext and then calculate the MAC for the ciphertext. With E&M, the ciphertext and the MAC are calculated in parallel from the same plaintext and often with the same key. Finally, with MtE, the MAC is calculated, appended to the plaintext, and the result is then encrypted.

The encrypted payload must be accompanied by an unencrypted message header and, possibly, a trailer in various messaging protocols. The family of methods where part of the message is sent in the clear, but the overall message is signed to ensure its integrity is called *authenticated encryption with associated data (AEAD)*.

1.9.6 Galois/Counter mode

One authenticated encryption mode is the *Galois/Counter Mode (GCM)* [26]. It works with a symmetric algorithm on 128-bit blocks, such as AES, and contains two functions, encryption and signature.

The encryption function has the advantage of allowing parallelization. Rather than encrypting each block with the underlying symmetric algorithm and chaining the result, the algorithm works as follows. Assume K is the key, IV is the initialization vector, M_i is the cleartext, and C_i is the desired ciphertext.

1. IV is encrypted using K to obtain the encryption mask: $X = E_K(IV)$.

2. The mask is XORed with the cleartext chunk: $C_i = M_i \oplus X$.

3. The least significant 32 bits of the IV are treated as a counter and increased by 1 for the next chunk. In case of an overflow, the lower 4 bytes wrap to zero.

4. The process continues for the next chunk.

Since the IV counter values are predictable, the encryption can commence in parallel for multiple input blocks.

The encryption function gives this mode the "counter" part of its name. The "Galois" part comes from its authentication function, *GHASH*. The exact computation relies on polynomial arithmetics over the $GF(2^{128})$ final field and is beyond the scope of this book. However, at a high level, the idea is as follows:

1. A point H is calculated by encrypting a zero input block with the key K.

2. The ciphertext and the additional authentication data are concatenated with their lengths.

3. The concatenated blocks are seen as coefficients of a polynomial.

4. The value of the polynomial at the point H is calculated and used as the authentication value of the message.

The GCM algorithm is sometimes used for authentication only. In that case, it is referred to as *GMAC*.

1.10 Randomness and Key Derivation

A poor or predictable key selection can undermine even a very strong algorithm. Each bit of the key that the attacker can predict by analyzing previous keys reduces the overall keyspace in half.

Therefore, the strength of the key generation is a critical part of any cryptographic solution.

In theory, the ideal key is a perfectly random sequence of bits or a random number. A random number generator would produce numbers that are distributed uniformly (i.e., each value has an equal probability of being output by the generator) and independently (i.e., knowing a previous value does not help predict the next value).

However, computers are by design deterministic and are built to produce outputs that are as predictable as possible. Therefore, without special hardware, a computer cannot produce a truly random sequence of bits. Luckily, this is not critical for cryptography: a computer cannot practically work with a truly unbreakable cipher, too, and the defining characteristic is just the computational difficulty of a possible attack.

Therefore, a deterministic *pseudo-random function* (*PRF*) is used in computing. A pseudo-random function can be computed effectively, and no efficient algorithm can distinguish between the PRF output and that of a truly random sequence.

The practice of applying cryptography often requires a reproducible generation of one or more keys out of a particular input which on its own may not be suitable as an encryption key for a particular algorithm. For instance, an elliptic curve Diffie-Helman scheme may use 168-bit values while the encryption algorithm for the data is a 192-bit AES. Alternatively, derivation of several keys from a single secret value may be required for a particular solution, as with AEAD (see *Section 1.9.5 Authenticated encryption*).

Initially, the recommended action in such circumstances was to pad the shared secret value to the necessary length, then XOR it with different values to derive specific keys from it. This approach is often called the *variant* approach, with the pre-defined XOR masks being the variants, and it was used, for instance, to represent encrypted keys (see *Section 5.3.1 X9.17 and variant formats*), to derive encryption and authentication keys for a key block (see *Section 5.3.2 Key block*), and to derive keys as part of the DUKPT protocol (see *Section 5.4 Derived Unique Key Per Transaction (DUKPT)*).

Later, the key derivation process was augmented and standardized in the form of *key derivation functions* (*KDF*) [27]. The KDF relies on a pseudo-random function as its main working component.

1.10.1 NIST 800-108 key derivation functions

As it turns out, both TDES and AES are valid pseudo-random functions when used in the CMAC mode (see *Section 1.9 Message Authentication Codes*) and are recommended in this quality by NIST [27, 28].

The standard KDF assumes that a pseudo-random function takes a key and an input value as its inputs. The PRF is invoked iteratively and in a particular order, and its outputs are concatenated until the desired key length is reached.

The KDF has three modes: counter mode, feedback mode, and double-pipeline iteration mode.

In the counter mode, the input of the PRF function includes a counter value which increases by one with each call. In the feedback mode, the output of the previous call to the PRF function becomes part of the input of the following invocation of the PRF function in addition to the counter. Finally, with the double-pipeline mode, the PRF function is invoked twice: first to generate a sequence of secret values that becomes part of the input for the second invocation of the PRF function, which finally outputs the key.

Note that the counter and the PRF outputs form only part of the input in all cases.

In the domain of payments, only the counter mode of the KDF is widely used. Furthermore, in some instances, the requirement for the pseudorandom function is slightly relaxed for the sake of speed of implementation.

In the counter mode, the input to the PRF function contains the following elements:

■ The counter itself.

■ *Label* – a string that identifies the purpose for the derived material. For example, data encryption or data authentication.

■ A zero separator byte.

■ *Context* – a string that defines information regarding the derived key. For example, it may contain the details of the algorithm that will be using the derived key.

■ The length, in bits, of the derived key.

The data is concatenated and fed into the pseudo-random function, using the secret as the key. The process is repeated until the PRF produces enough bits.

This method is implemented with TR-31 key block representations of encrypted keys (see *Section 5.3.2 Key Block*).

1.10.2 *ConcatKDF key derivation function*

The ConcatKDF key derivation function was designed as part of the NIST SP 800-56 standard for key agreement schemes [29] and predated NIST SP 800-108 [27].

The ConcatKDF key derivation is based on a shared secret, Z, which was established using a key exchange process such as Diffie-Hellman or elliptic curve Diffie-Hellman (see *Sections 1.5.2 Diffie-Hellman key exchange (DHE)* and *1.6.2 Elliptic curve Diffie-Hellman (ECDH)*).

The method uses the notion of OtherInfo, which roughly corresponds to the label and context information of the NIST 800-108 key derivation process [27]. The OtherInfo value contains the following subfields:

- *AlgorithmID* – an identifier of the algorithm.

- *PartyUInfo* – information about the initiating party. It has the format of length concatenated with the data.

- *PartyVInfo* – information about the recipient party. It has the same format of length concatenated with the data as PartyUI Info.

- *SuppPubInfo* and *SuppPrivInfo* – additional mutually known public and private information as a raw value.

The method relies on a hash function, H, and operates as follows:

1. A 32-bit counter *cnt* is initialized to the value of 1.

2. The counter is concatenated with the desired output key length *kl* and with the *OtherInfo* data to obtain the hash function input I: $I = cnt \parallel kl \parallel OtherInfo$.

3. The result is hashed using H to obtain a portion of the output key: $R_{cnt} = H(I)$.

4. The counter is increased by 1, and the method iterates from step 2 until the total length of R_i has reached the target length.

5. The trailing bits are truncated if the desired key length is not an integer number of hash output blocks.

1.11 Key Trust and Key Certificates

Cryptographic signatures allow a delegation of trust, among other valuable features.

For example, consider the scenario of bank account access under the EU PSD2 Directive (see *Section 6.1 Payment Services Directive 2 (PSD2)*). Banks, of which in Europe there are thousands, are obliged to expose API to any of the hundreds or more payment service providers. The API access is granted to entities that possess a valid certificate. It is impractical to expect both the banks and the PSPs to whitelist such access individually.

Hence, the regulators in different EU countries have authorized a limited number of trusted entities to issue such certificates. Banks do not have to trust each of the PSPs; they just need to trust the issuing entity and make sure that the certificate is genuine.

The method works as follows: the issuing entity creates a pair of public/private keys and makes the public key generally available. A PSP requests a certificate from the entity, which signs it with its private key. Then, the bank

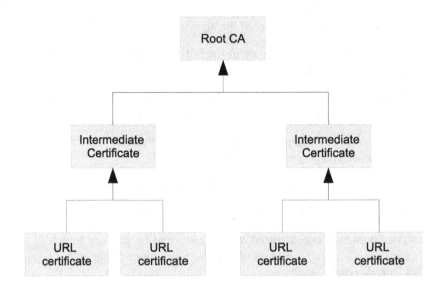

Figure 1.8: Key chain of trust.

just needs to validate the signature using a known public key to confirm that the certificate is valid.

An arrangement that binds public keys and their signatures to entities such as individuals or companies is called a *public key infrastructure (PKI)*.

It is possible to create a hierarchy with arbitrary many levels of trust, or at least as many as is practically useable. Such a hierarchy is best presented in the form of a tree (see Figure 1.8).

The authority that needs to be explicitly trusted and does not derive the trust elsewhere is called the root or *certification authority (CA)*. While keys from lower levels of the key trust hierarchy can be validated automatically, the public keys of the root authorities must be deployed as part of the solution that relies on them.

For example, root certificates are deployed as part of operating systems and internet browsers. With these trusted certificates deployed, individual TLS certificates can be recognized and validated automatically. It is worth noting that typically, CAs operate via intermediate certificates, and for a clean deployment to validate certificates successfully, the intermediaries have to be present as well.

The standard that governs TLS certificates is ITU-T X.509 [30], it is identical to ISO/IEC 9594-8 [31]. The X.509 format has many details regarding possible certificate fields.

For each certificate, there is the *issuer* and the *subject*. The subject is the entity that requests the certificate, such as a website or an API endpoint. The issuer is the entity that signs the certificate.

To obtain a certificate, the applicant (the future subject of the certificate) creates a *certificate request* (*CSR*) and sends it to the certificate authority, which signs it and returns the certificate. The most common format for certificate requests is defined in PKCS #10 [32], and its filename typically has extensions of .pem, .cer, .crt, or .der.

Before generating the CSR file, the applicant must generate a public/private key pair and then sign the certificate with the private key. The CA will sign the certificate with theirs, and during the TLS handshake (see *Section 4.1 Transport Layer Security (TLS)*), the private key of the applicant will be required to confirm the ownership of the certificate.

The certificate request contains details such as the domain and the organization name, the organizational unit, address, and email. Its filename extension is often .csr.

The certificate authority can then use these details to perform several types of validation, from the more superficial *domain validation* (confirming ownership of the domain) to the *extended validation*, which covers legal business verification.

Since the private key must be retained and used alongside the certificate to confirm its validity as part of the TLS protocol, it is usually kept in a secure keystore on the relevant server. The PKCS #12 standard defines a secure file format that can store multiple cryptographic objects in a single file [33]. This format is often used for such a keystore. Its filename extension is .p12 or .pfx.

The certificate authorities manage *certificate revocation lists* (*CRL*). Such lists contain certificates that had been revoked or put on hold prior to their expiration date. The PKCS #7 standard defines a format that is frequently used to contain CRLs [34]. While an online protocol, OCSP (see below), is gradually replacing CRLs, specific solutions may have to continue relying on this method.

The *Online Certificate Status Protocol* (*OCSP*) is used to obtain a particular certificate's status [35]. A CA usually sets up an OCSP server, and its address is available as part of the certificate. The OCSP responses from CAs are signed by the CA private key, and the requesting entity can validate the signature using CA's public key. Modern browsers have the OCSP support built-in and use it by default.

The file formats mentioned above and the OCSP protocol rely on ASN.1 [36–46]. The OpenSSL library provides a comprehensive set of tools to generate, manipulate, and sign certificates, certificate requests, and certificate files and read and write ASN.1 encodings.

Chapter 2

Understanding Payments

2.1 Introduction

Payment is the economically essential process of making a due return for goods or services rendered. As people sold goods and provided services way before the invention of the alphabet, this is one of the eldest processes known to man.

Initially, the payment was by barter; a measure of grain or livestock[1] addressed the need for a unit of account. As the range of the trade increased, metals came into use, and minted coins followed.

At a certain point, notes and cheques (which, in the form of IOUs, existed at least since the clay tablets) became a significant payment instrument alongside the coin and the bullion. Then, with time, paper displaced metal until, at some point, computers and electronic communication means became affordable. This way, money – essentially just an idea – finally broke free from any material embodiment to which it formerly had to be tied.

Throughout history, payment has been a prime target for fraud and counterfeiting. And with fraud and counterfeits came the counter measures. One of the most famous is probably the anecdotal story of Archimedes inventing the eponymous law: tasked with identifying whether a metal object was pure gold, Archimedes made the reasonable choice of taking a bath instead. Being a keen

---

[1]The interest as we know it is a future contract on the increase of a flock: an owner would lend out their sheep to a herder, who would commit to return the original headcount plus a few extras, keeping whatever extra animal yield his skill would provide.

DOI: 10.1201/9781003371366-2

observer, he noted water displacement, invented a method to identify the composition of an alloy, and gave the citizens of Syracuse a show along the way.

Electronic payment methods face the same malicious intent, but, naturally, the attack and defense methods are quite different.

Luckily for the payment industry, the military perfected the art of protecting sensitive communications over an untrusted channel way before computing machines became available to bankers and financiers.

At the same time, the versatile nature of computers enabled the evolution and proliferation of various payment methods.

Interbank electronic transfers were probably the first; card payments switched to electronic rails afterward – and then, with the rise of the Internet, online payment methods came into being. Initially, just a means to invoke other payment methods (trigger a card payment or a bank transfer), online payment mechanisms evolved into staged wallets and, finally, cryptocurrencies.

Different electronic payment methods have different vulnerabilities and require specific means of protection. However, the underlying technology of deterministic computers and computer networks is the same; furthermore, all payment methods fulfill the same function and hence share the same core features.

Each payment method requires the availability of balance on some form of an account; each payment method requires a payment credential that will confirm the payee's rights to manipulate funds on that account; that credential has to be validated by a counterpart (or, in case of cryptocurrencies, by a network of counterparts), and in the process, it has to be transmitted securely.

While most electronic payment methods exist purely online, at least before the advent of the smartphone, card payment methods have the longest track record of large-scale physical presence in the brick-and-mortar world. Many vulnerabilities were found, exploited, and fixed for over 70 years, bringing card payments to the cutting edge of technology relevant to this book.

2.2   Payment Methods

2.2.1   Card payments

The first payment card was made of cardboard and belonged to the newly established Diners club. Its function was to facilitate monthly payments for business lunches and dinners – member restaurants wrote down the card numbers and amounts due. At the end of the month, the card company collected the money from cardholders and remitted the funds to participating businesses.

The card company, including the infrastructure and the operational rules to which members commit upon joining, is called a *card scheme*.

There are two principal classes of card schemes: *open* or *four-party schemes* and *closed* or *three-party schemes*, although the line is somewhat blurred. In

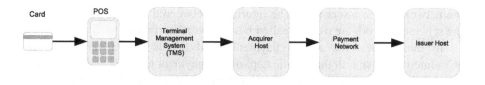

Figure 2.1: Flow of a payment transaction.

closed schemes, the scheme itself provides service to cardholders and to businesses that accept its cards. With open schemes, multiple institutions can service cardholders and merchants. Institutions (usually banks) that service cardholders are called *issuers* since they issue payment instruments. Institutions that service merchants are called *acquirers* since they acquire card payments. Of course, an institution can be, and usually is, both[2].

In addition to the major participants such as issuers and acquirers, there are many other players in the card payments ecosystem. Some simply provide services to other entities. For example, organizations that resell payment processing services and provide customer support are called *independent sales organizations* or *ISOs*.

Others have a technology platform that participates in the payment processing flow. The most generic name for entities of that sort is *payment service providers* (*PSPs*). In some cases, when the PSP is also handling payouts to merchants, the term used is *payment facilitators* (*PFs* or *PayFacs*).

Payment cards are used in two major scenarios, depending on whether the card is physically present at the point of sale. Accordingly, these are *card present* and *card not present*.

Today, a smartphone or a wearable device can replace a plastic card. For simplicity, we will use the term *card* to denote all such objects or devices.

The devices used to capture card payments are often called *point-of-sale* devices or *POS*. This term is imprecise since a cashier supports many additional functions in addition to capturing card payments. An alternative term for such a device is *pin entry device* (*PED*), *card reader*, *point of interaction* (*POI*), or *PIN pad*. All, too, err on the side of simplicity.

The flow of a payment transaction is shown in Figure 2.1. The POS devices interact with a *terminal management system* (*TMS*), which connects to the acquirer host and through it to the scheme network. The transactions flow through

---

[2]Prima facie, open schemes introduce extra competing players and have a more complicated ecosystem than closed schemes. However, in reality open schemes completely dominate the card payments market, leaving only single-digit market shares to the closed schemes.

the network to the issuer host. The interfaces between the TMS, the hosts, and the scheme network are usually called *host-to-host* interfaces.

In most cases, for a card payment, card details are captured on the eCommerce website, in the mobile app, or at a payment terminal and forwarded through several intermediaries to the card scheme network and from there to the issuer. The issuer analyzes the details and decides whether to approve or decline the request.

In some cases, the issuer can delegate this decision. For instance, major schemes support a version of stand-in processing. In case of issuer unavailability or according to a rule, the scheme can approve or decline the request and only notify the issuer about the decision made.

The eCommerce website will not connect directly to a card scheme network; in most cases, the websites do not connect directly to acquiring hosts. A software component, called a *payment gateway*, usually captures the online transaction and then forwards it to a back-end processor.

With chip-based cards, the issuer can configure (*personalize*) the chip on the card to authorize certain transactions without communication to the issuer, simply based on the exchange of messages between the terminal and the card.

Depending on the scheme protocol, the request might have to be followed with a clearing message or a clearing file to perform the actual financial operation. The clearing message may contain additional details regarding the transaction that were unavailable during authorization. There might be just the clearing record in case of offline authorization (when the terminal authorized the transaction based on its exchange with the chip on the card).

During an online transaction performed via the browser, it is enough to simply pass the card details to the payment gateway (the specialized software for processing payments) to perform the transaction. However, based on the security needs of the transaction, the website may decide or even have to redirect the user to their issuer's specialized system for some extra authentication steps, upon completion of which the user will be redirected back.

Examples of card schemes include Visa, Mastercard, UnionPay (four-party schemes), American Express, Discover/Diners, and JCB (three-party schemes).

2.2.2 *Bank transfers*

Card payments are not the only method to transfer money between the customer and the merchant. Online and in-store methods for the initiation of wire transfers also exist.

Unlike card payment methods, where the scheme or member institutions aggregate remittances for participating businesses, most bank transfer methods remit the merchant's funds per transaction.

Such a payment usually consists of a form of authentication of the account owner, followed by payment authorization. Both authentication and authorization can happen either as part of the browser-based flow or through an out-of-band process, typically involving a mobile app or phone.

In the first case, the account owner may be redirected to the bank's page or frame, authorize the payment, and then sent back to the store website. Alternatively, a push notification can be sent to the account owner's phone, asking to authorize the operation in the bank's app.

The transfers work both ways: it is possible to initiate a credit transfer (send funds from the customer's account to the store) or grant debit permission (allow the store to debit the account for a particular amount immediately or in the future).

Some bank transfer payment methods support payment at the store alongside online channels.

There are two major mechanisms to achieve that. The store can present a link (a QR code or identifier) and check and confirm wire transfers. Alternatively, the store can initiate a payment request with the customer's bank. The customer then can confirm the payment by keying in a one-time authorization code into the terminal or telling the clerk.

Examples of bank transfer payment methods include iDEAL, Blik, and Sofort.

2.2.3 *Digital wallets*

A digital wallet can either carry its own balance (constituting what EU legislation dubs *e-money*, an electronic payment method of which it is the issuer) or protect a credential of another payment method.

In the second case, the credential can be a card, an access token to a bank account, or a private key of a cryptocurrency.

All these cases share the same security challenges and, with the partial exception of cryptocurrency, use cryptographic methods similarly.

2.2.4 *Cryptocurrencies*

Other payment methods mentioned here require cryptography in security protocols but can perfectly function without any. If an algorithm used by card payments becomes obsolete because of a vulnerability or quantum supremacy, schemes can overcome this with a slight change in a specific protocol.

Cryptocurrencies differ in that, by design, they rely on cryptographic algorithms to work. So a discovered vulnerability will mandate a significant reengineering of a cryptocurrency, which is not always possible due to the distributed and anarchical nature of the crypto coins.

Cryptocurrencies are a fascinating topic with many solutions and many developments, but most of them are beyond the scope of this book. To process a payment with a cryptocurrency, one need not understand every possible detail of its consensus mechanism nor be able to develop smart contracts. Hence, we will illustrate the principles of blockchain technology and cryptocurrencies, following the structure of bitcoin but not in every detail.

There are two mechanisms that power cryptocurrencies: hash functions and asymmetric cryptography. The former ensures that the underlying blockchain can work; the latter allows authentication and authorization of payments over it.

2.2.4.1 Blockchain

Blockchain is a method to chain blocks of transactions. It is unrelated to the CBC (cipher block chaining) except in name. It is also called *distributed ledger technology (DLT)*.

Imagine a ledger to which users write transactions between some accounts. Once we have accumulated a certain number of transactions or a predefined time has elapsed, we sign off the block by computing a hash of its contents. We then start a new block by writing this hash value first and adding the transactions to the block after that (see Figure 2.2).

Since our ledger is distributed by nature, it is public, and many entities (or *nodes*) hold its copies. Due to the hashing and chaining of the hashes, an entity cannot falsify a historical transaction without a trace: the block's hash will necessarily change, the next block will have to be modified, and its hash will change too, and so on. Hence, to modify a historical transaction, it is necessary to recalculate the entire chain of blocks after the one where it belonged.

Besides malicious intent, such a disparity in the blockchain structure can occur for technical reasons, such as a network split, which is not uncommon in distributed systems.

As the classic blockchain implementations were designed to be distributed and open to anyone, there was a need for a mechanism to resolve such disparities

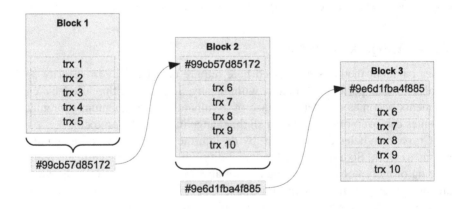

Figure 2.2: Blocks in a blockchain.

and protect the system from bad players. Such a mechanism is called a *consensus mechanism.*

Several alternatives to the consensus mechanism design exist today, but the *proof-of-work* is the oldest and the most widespread. Its goal is to artificially increase the computational complexity of hashing when signing the block while leaving the validation of the hash computationally easy.

With this method, in case of a dispute, the combined computational power of each side of the argument will resolve it. If we assume that the combined computational power of all participating nodes is significant and the power is distributed more or less evenly among the nodes, this is not a bad solution.

If a part of the network splits off, the majority of the nodes will force their version of the ledger on the minority; if there is malicious intent by a portion of the network, the majority that is not part of the plot will neutralize it.

One way to increase the complexity of computing a hash while leaving its validation unaffected is to add a salt value to it and enforce a constraint on the resulting value of the hash (see also *Section 1.7 Hash Functions*). Participating nodes have the liberty of adding a *nonce* (a number that is passed along openly as part of each block in the blockchain). However, to successfully sign off a block, a node needs to make sure the hash, if viewed as a large number, complies with a demand of being smaller than a particular threshold (or starts with a particular number of zero bytes).

As it is impossible to predict the nonce with which the hash will comply with this requirement, nodes must "brute-force" nonce values by trying to add them to the block and hash the result. This process can be optimized to make better use of the hardware, moved to specialized hardware such as GPUs, parallelized, and scaled, but it is still computationally hard. The process requires an investment of computing power and electricity, and at the same time, it is essential for the proper functioning of the blockchain network. To provide an economic reward for network participants, bitcoin and some other protocols compensate the nodes that succeed in signing a block with some amount of the currency, and the overall process is called mining.

To perform operations over a blockchain, consumers submit transactions to a pool from which the mining nodes retrieve them, pack them into blocks, and sign them. Many blockchain implementations have a mechanism for specifying a fee that will be paid by the submitting consumer to the mining node in case of a successful signing of the transaction into a block.

2.2.4.2 Payment over blockchain

As mentioned above, blockchain tracks transactions between accounts rather than balances. While the consensus mechanisms make sure no mining node goes rogue, the users seem to be able to submit any transaction they like, moving funds from one account to another.

With traditional currency, banks are responsible for authenticating account owners and confirming the validity of payment credentials. The authentication also has to be delegated with the distributed ledger technology, so the solution relies on public/private cryptography and a simple principle: if there are no trusted entities to validate credentials, everyone must be able to validate credentials.

Cryptocurrencies rely on public/private cryptography to achieve that. The "account number" is the public key, and each transaction on the ledger is a funds transfer between two public keys. A public address can receive funds from anyone. However, to send money from an address, a user needs to know the private key and prove the knowledge by using it to sign sign the transaction.

Therefore, holders of cryptocurrencies no more hold a valuable asset than they do with bank accounts. Instead, they possess a cryptographic key that allows issuing outbound transfers from a particular address.

Since there is no central authority or deposit insurance, and as blockchain transactions are irreversible, losing a private key means losing access to the funds on a particular address. Services, software, or hardware that securely store these keys are called *crypto wallets*. Such a wallet can be *cold*[3], storing the private keys offline, or *hot* – keeping the keys in a manner that requires an internet connection.

Other than the cornerstone role of cryptography in the architecture of the public cryptocurrency infrastructure, securing hot crypto wallets is not radically different from securing any other online payment method. Perhaps the only essential difference is how attractive crypto wallets are in light of the ease of transferring the funds away to an anonymous account – an operation that is considerably more difficult with bank accounts or cards.

2.3   Security of Card Payments

To debit an account, the only thing issuer needs to know is its number (also known as *PAN* or *primary account number*)[4]. The number itself is, therefore, sensitive and must be kept secret. However, it can be used to perform transactions unlimitedly once stolen – until the issuer notices and blocks further transactions.

As payment technology evolved and usage scenarios proliferated, criminals came up with new and inventive ways of stealing money using cards, and the industry responded with countermeasures.

There are three areas where methods to protect card payments are applied. These are card authentication, cardholder verification, and data security. In layman's terms, these are protocols and procedures to ensure that the card is genuine, that the cardholder is indeed one performing the transaction, and that the sensitive data (PAN and additional authentication values) is safe in the process.

---

[3]The simplest cold wallet is a piece of paper with the owner's private key written on it.

[4]Non-card payment methods share the same security challenges as card payments or other online or mobile applications.

2.3.1 Card authentication

Card authentication methods focus on creating obstacles for making and using counterfeit cards. Initially, the industry relied on holograms to be verified by store clerks. With the introduction of the magnetic stripe technology, a special value, CVC/CVV_1, was embedded – hidden – among other card data on the magnetic stripe.

When electronic commerce gained enough volume to cause significant losses due to fraud, a similar mechanism – CVV_2 – was extended to online payments.

The next – and, for now, the last – advancement in card authentication happened with the introduction of the EMV technology. The smart card on the chip allowed the implementation of card authentication based on cryptography, providing perhaps the most reliable protection from counterfeiting to date.

2.3.2 Cardholder verification

Cardholder verification methods ensure that the actual cardholder is presenting the card and performing the transaction.

In the card-present world, the authentication was initially done by visually comparing signatures on the card and the slip. Then, the ability to enter a PIN code for a magnetic stripe card was introduced (primarily for ATMs). With the EMV technology, a chip was powerful enough to validate the PIN code at the point of sale, and so the PIN code became the widespread method for cardholder verification. Finally, many smartphones and wearables which began supporting EMV contactless payments were also capable of biometric identification of the cardholder. With that, card-present payments started to rely on consumer devices for cardholder verification.

In the online world, the industry has initially relied on CVV_2 as proof that the person on the other end of the internet connection indeed holds the card in their hand. This method (a possession factor) was supplemented in some countries by the *Address Verification Service* (*AVS*), which added a knowledge factor – the consumer would provide their billing address, and the card's issuer would try to match it to the address on record.

Then, 3D Secure, a method for authentication of the cardholder by the issuer, appeared. With 3D Secure, the cardholder would be redirected to a webpage hosted by the card issuer, enter whatever identification details the issuer required, and then redirected back to the online store with cryptographic evidence of the successful authentication. The online store should then send that evidence to the issuer for final approval alongside other transaction details.

The method was later augmented and redesigned as the EMV 3DS 2.0 open standard, supporting, in addition to the above, other authentication scenarios such as frictionless flows, push notifications to the consumer's phone, and a much better handheld UI support. For more details, see *Chapter 4 Securing the Network*.

2.3.3 Data security

Early electronic terminals were designed and deployed assuming that communication lines to processing centers were safe from eavesdropping or hard to tap.

However, with online payments, the interception of PAN and CVV_2 values quickly became a reality. The internet industry responded by creating several revisions of a "Secure Sockets Layer" or SSL, supplanted by TLS (Transport Layer Security).

For the protection of data, the card industry has instituted the PCI SSC (Payment Card Industry Security Standards Council), which develops and maintains a family of standards such as PCI DSS (Data Security Standard), PCI PIN, PCI PTS (PIN Transaction Security), and PCI P2PE (Point-to-Point Encryption).

The latter, PCI P2PE, had appeared because of the increasing need to protect data in transit in the card-present world, especially as wireless networks came into wide use.

Chapter 3

Securing the Plastic: Magnetic Stripe and EMV

3.1 Overview

Prior to the introduction of EMV, the magnetic stripe technology relied on three relatively simple measures: visual elements on the physical card itself, a signature on the back, and the CVC/CVV_1 value embedded into the track data.

The EMV technology added several much more advanced card authentication and cardholder verification methods, to which the contactless technology added relatively little. The technology relies on communications between the terminal and the chip embedded into the plastic. The chip is capable of cryptographic calculations, as well as the terminal. Furthermore, the chip can store secret keys securely.

The chip allows many opportunities for improved security of payments. For instance, the terminal can use cryptography to establish the chip's authenticity. The chip and the terminal can exchange messages to approve the transaction offline. The chip can generate an encrypted message to the issuer and then confirm the authenticity of the issuer's response. Finally, the chip can independently

DOI: 10.1201/9781003371366-3

validate the cardholder's PIN without sending dedicated messages through the payment network.

The detailed steps of the card interaction with the terminal are pretty complex and lengthy, and most do not relate directly to security or cryptography. An introductory overview is given in "Acquiring Card Payments." [47] Also, the full standard is available for free from the EMVCo website [48].

EMV transactions happen in two ways: either by inserting the card into the terminal, i.e., via an electrical contact and in a time-unbound manner, or by tapping the card or mobile device on a compatible contactless reader.

The original EMV standard was contact-only, and contactless methods gradually emerged several years later. Hence, the latter built off the former; furthermore, several bodies made concurrent attempts at defining a contactless protocol, and so, multiple concurrent implementations, also called Kernels, exist in the EMV Contactless standard.

However, all security mechanisms in the Contactless kernels are a subset of the original EMV standard; therefore, describing them for EMV Contact will cover all potential implementation needs for the Contactless protocol.

3.2   Definitions and Legacy Mechanisms

Before diving into the chip-specific methods for card protection, it is prudent first to overview the methods used for the magnetic stripe. There are three good reasons for it: the CVV mechanism is in wide use in online transactions; the magnetic stripe is still present as a fallback option and will continue to exist for a while; and finally, the chip on the card simulates data from the magnetic stripe and returns it as part of its message exchange with the POS.

The magnetic stripe of a payment card stores data physically according to ISO/IEC 7811 [49]. It can contain up to three *tracks*, Track 1, Track 2, and Track 3. ISO/IEC standard 7813 [50] describes the structure of Tracks 1 and 2, while ISO/IEC 4909 [51] describes Track 3. The structure of these tracks can also be found in the "Acquiring Card Payments" book [47].

Since Track 3 is not widespread anymore, and the focus of this chapter is security, we will just highlight the significant features shared by tracks 1 and 2.

The card number is called the *primary account number* (*PAN*). It can vary in total length from 13 to 19 digits, with the last digit in most cases being the Luhn check digit of the rest of the number (see *Appendix A.6 Luhn's Algorithm*).

PAN's first 3 to 9 digits are the *bank identification number* (*BIN*) and allow identification of the bank that has issued this card.

Since it is possible to re-issue a card with the same account number but a different expiry date, a card also carries a *card sequence number* or *CSN*.

The PAN and the card's expiry date are present on Tracks 1 and 2. In addition, the two tracks contain the *service code*, a three-digit code that describes various usage limitations for the card. Its most frequent use today is to indicate the presence of a chip on the card. When a card with such a service code is swiped through its magstripe reader, a supporting terminal will prompt the cardholder to insert the chip or tap the card on the contactless reader instead.

There are at least three possible fraud scenarios: modifying the expiry date, modifying the service code, or constructing the track data from stolen partial information (e.g., the PAN).

Both Track 1 and Track 2 allocate several digits for the so-called "*discretionary data*" to allow for a digital signature. These are decimal digits rather than any binary value since Track 2 encoding supports a limited set of characters. Card schemes and issuers can decide which values to embed there and the exact location. Specifically, the digits of the card verification value (CVV) or card verification code (CVC) are stored in the discretionary data parts of Tracks 1 and 2.

With the spread of online payments, schemes use the same mechanism to generate the CVV_2 value that is printed on the card. The two CVV values sign different service codes to prevent the use of online data for in-store payments and vice versa. The Track 1/Track 2 CVV uses the actual service code of the card, while the CVV_2 value uses the service code of 000.

The other use for discretionary data follows from some factors in the world of card payment that require certain flexibility for validation of the cardholder's PIN. On the one hand, the PIN must be kept secret, and the issuer cannot entrust it to a third party. On the other hand, the issuer often delegates transaction processing to either a processing center or to the scheme's "stand-in" facilities[1]. To meet these constraints, issuers can opt to use *PIN verification value* (*PVV*).

3.2.1 CVV/CVC calculation and CVKs

The CVV/CVC calculation generates a 3- or 4-digit numeric code from the PAN, expiry date, and the service code. The algorithm requires two 64-bit DES keys (i.e., with an odd parity bit in each byte), K_A and K_B, called the *Card Verification Keys* (*CVK*).

The input data is first arranged into two blocks, B_1 and B_2. The blocks are binary-coded decimals.

Block B_1 consists of the last 16 digits of the PAN. If the PAN is shorter than 16 digits, it is padded from the left with zeroes to the full length of 16 digits or 8 bytes. Block B_2 consists of the four digits of the expiry date (2 digits of the month and 2 digits of the year), followed by the service code and zero-padded from the right to the full length.

---

[1]A scheme stand-in system processes the transactions when the issuer is unavailable or explicitly delegates the processing for particular transaction criteria. The stand-in maintains counters for accumulated amounts and can approve or decline transactions.

For example, the PAN number of 98765432109876, with the expiry date of October 2025 and service code of 101, will be represented as $B_1 = 0098765432109876$, $B_2 = 1025101000000000$.

Then, the flow is as follows:

1. B_1 is encrypted using the DES algorithm with K_A.

2. The result is XOR-ed with B_2.

3. The result of the XOR operation is encrypted using the TDES algorithm in the EDE pattern with K_B.

4. The outcome is decimalized (i.e., the decimal digits are extracted from the result in a particular order, see *Appendix A.7 Decimalization*).

The further use of the outcome depends on the type of the CVV. CVV_1 will be embedded in the discretionary data section of Tracks 1 and 2 on the magnetic stripe. CVV_2 will be printed on the card for online and telephone purchases.

In the case of a chip-based card, the third CVV value called *iCVV* is calculated with a service code value of 999. Since the chip on the card returns a "mock" Track 2 value as part of the exchange with the terminal, it must contain valid discretionary data. However, if this Track 2 value is intercepted, the fraudster will be able to use it neither for a magnetic stripe counterfeit (since the service code signed by the CVV on the magstripe reflects the permitted functions and differs from 999) nor for online purchases (since the CVV_2 value reflects the service code of 000).

An example C implementation of CVV calculation can be found in src/payments.c, function compute_cvv().

3.2.2 *PVV, PVKs, and PVKI*

PVV is a method for validating PIN values that allows delegation of the validation to third parties without compromising the values themselves and is also lightweight enough to be used by issuer banks.

To compute the PVV, the issuer generates two 64-bit DES keys called the *PIN verification key (PVK)* pair, PVK-A, and PVK-B. There usually is more than one pair of keys in use in real-life implementations. The *PVK index (PVKI)* indicates the PVK pair in use.

The flow to compute the PVV is as follows:

1. The 11 rightmost digits of the PAN except the Luhn check digit are placed in nibbles 1-11 of the input vector.

2. The PVKI is placed in nibble 12 of the input vector.

3. The first 4 digits of the PIN are placed in positions 13 to 16.

4. The input vector is encrypted using the TDES algorithm in the EDE pattern with PVK-A and PVK-B.

5. The result is decimalized, and four digits are extracted.

The PVV and the PVKI are then embedded into the discretionary data area of the magnetic stripe tracks. The probability of a wrong PIN yielding the correct PVV is negligible.

The method has the obvious drawback of limiting the PIN to 4 meaningful digits. However, it has the advantage of greatly simplifying managing the PIN values.

With PVV, the issuer no longer needs to store encrypted PIN values for each cardholder. It is sufficient to generate the PVV, write it to the card, and discard the actual PIN, keeping only the PVK pair. It is much easier to manage and protect a handful of PVK values than a million encrypted PIN values.

Furthermore, by (securely) communicating the PVK values to the schemes, the issuer can delegate PIN verification to the network, offloading their own systems.

Of course, in case of a compromise of a PVK pair, all cards that use it must be replaced. Another disadvantage of this method besides the PIN length is that the PIN is immutable once written to the card.

An example C implementation of PVV generation can be found in `src/payments.c`, function `compute_pvv()`.

3.3   EMV Transaction Flow

The EMV transaction flow has multiple steps, not all of them involving cryptography.

The EMV contact flow [52–55], built under the assumption of time-unlimited interaction with the cardholder, is the fullest from the point of view of invoked EMV commands and performed actions. Hence, to understand the cryptography aspects of an EMV payment, this is the flow to start.

In general, the chip on the card contains *applications*. There can be many applications on the same chip, including those unrelated to payments. At the very least, there will be one application of the card scheme, but a card can contain applications from several schemes or several applications for the same scheme.

The interaction between the card and the terminal is a series of requests from the terminal to which the card responds.

The important notion in this regard is the data format and the concept of *data object lists* (*DOLs*). Each data element in the EMV domain is assigned a unique tag value and listed in the EMV documentation. The data elements are represented in the *tag-length-value* (*TLV*) format, where the tag value is followed by the value length and then by the value itself.

The terminal and the card begin from the application selection, matching schemes and applications that are supported on the terminal to counterparts on the card. In some scenarios, the terminal may ask the cardholder to choose the application (e.g., debit or credit payment).

At later stages of the flow, both terminal and the card will need to decide how to proceed with the transaction, if at all. For that, the terminal needs to learn more about the card, and, conversely, the card needs to learn details about the terminal and the transaction it will be requested to perform.

Once the terminal retrieves the card data, it can perform a card authentication. It is an optional step as card authentication can be combined with one of the later steps of the transaction.

After that, the terminal and the card negotiate the cardholder verification method and execute the chosen method.

The terminal and the card then negotiate the method to confirm the transaction, including whether to involve the card issuer. The card and the terminal can negotiate a transaction result (approval or decline) without involving the issuer. Alternatively, an *application request cryptogram* (*ARQC*) may be sent to the issuer, and the card uses the issuer's response (*application response cryptogram* or *ARPC*) to authenticate the issuer.

The issuer may transmit some commands to the card that the latter will execute.

Finally, according to the protocol, the card should produce a transaction certificate confirming the transaction's conclusion. In practice, once the authorization request to the issuer has been approved, many implementations opt not to transmit that final certificate.

3.4   Card Authentication

There are three methods for card authentication called *static data authentication* (*SDA*), *dynamic data authentication* (*DDA*), and *combined data authentication* (*CDA*). They differ as follows.

The terminal performs static data authentication based on fields it has read from the card application. It is the weaker form of authentication in the standard.

For dynamic data authentication, the terminal performs the static data authentication step and also an additional message exchange with the card in the form of a challenge and a response.

Finally, the combined data authentication is a form of dynamic data authentication with the message exchange deferred to a later stage. Specifically, rather than performing a separate message exchange for the DDA, the terminal combines this message interchange with a request for the application cryptogram (see *3.4.4 Application Cryptograms and Issuer Authentication*).

With the static data authentication, the terminal retrieves a list of static fields, a public key, and the signature during the initial retrieval of card data. The terminal recovers and validates a public key (later on) using one of the card scheme certificates it has to hold and then uses the recovered value to validate the static data.

With the dynamic and combined data authentication, the terminal recovers and validates a public key and then sends data to the card. The data includes a random number, protecting the interaction from possible replay attacks. The card responds with a signature value that the terminal can validate using the recovered public key.

The dynamic/combined data authentication places more demand on the card's resources, requiring a more powerful chip.

Besides a difference in the process itself, the public keys with which the authentication is performed differ. For the static authentication process, the terminal recovers an *issuer public key*, which is signed with a card scheme key. For the dynamic authentication process, the terminal recovers the issuer key, then uses it to recover the *ICC public key*, which is individually generated per card.

3.4.1 Static data authentication

3.4.1.1 Key data format

The key recovery and validation are based on a pre-defined set of card scheme public keys, called *Certification Authority Public Keys*, which are pre-loaded into the terminals. Each CA public key is identified by the id of the EMV application and the public key index. It is the acquirer's responsibility to ensure these keys are always up to date according to the latest data from the relevant card schemes.

Although the EMV standard, in theory, allows support for other encryption algorithms, currently, the only public/private algorithm in use is RSA, and the hash function in use is SHA-1.

The issuer public key and the ICC public key are represented using the same format. However, the computation of the signature differs slightly.

Since the algorithm is RSA (see *1.5.1 RSA*), the keys are a pair of numbers: the modulus n and the public exponent e. The standard allows only two values for the public exponent, 3 and 0x10001. This rule applies to all keys, including the CA public keys.

The maximum length of the card scheme certificate is 248 bytes. The issuer public key modulus itself must be of the same length or shorter than the CA public key used to sign it. Assuming N_{CA} is the length of the CA public key, If the modulus is longer than $N_{CA} - 36$, it is broken into two parts: the Issuer Public Key Certificate and the Issuer Public Key Remainder. While the Issuer Public Key Certificate is encrypted, the Remainder is not.

The terminal reads from the card the following data to be able to recover the issuer public key: the CA public key index, the issuer public key certificate, the optional issuer public key remainder, and the issuer public key exponent.

3.4.1.2 Key recovery

The recovery of the issuer key value itself is straightforward. The terminal first locates the correct CA public key. This value is actually the modulus for the public exponent of the CA public key. The flow continues as follows:

The terminal decrypts the Issuer Public Key Certificate using the exponent and the modulus (raising the certificate to the power of the public exponent and computing the result modulo the modulus).

The decrypted result must always begin with the byte sentinel value of 0x6A and end with the value of 0xBC. If the decrypted value's first or last byte differs, the decryption (and the card authentication) has failed.

After stripping off the sentinels, the remaining data contains a header, followed by a chunk of the issuer public key, followed by a 20-byte hash value H. If the issuer's key length is less than $N_{CA} - 36$, the value will be right-padded with the value of 0xBB. If the length of the issuer's key is greater than $N_{CA} - 36$, it will be truncated, and the rest of the key will be provided as cleartext in the Issuer Public Key Remainder.

The header fields are listed in Figure 3.1. Note that the fields contain the issuer identifier, which should be cross-checked with the PAN to make sure the key fits it, and the certificate expiration date in the MMYY format, which should be earlier or equal to the current month and year.

At this point, the terminal has the two clear-text pieces of the issuer public key. Their simple concatenation will yield the key's modulus and complete the recovery.

The validation of the issuer public key follows its recovery. In order to validate the key, the terminal concatenates the recovered header value, appends the issuer public key remainder, if available, and finally appends the Issuer Public Key Exponent. Note that the length of the exponent is either 1 or 3 bytes. The result of the concatenation is fed into the SHA-1 hash function, which yields a 20-byte value, H'. This value must be identical to the value of H that was recovered during the previous step.

Note that the signature includes the first few digits of the card number and the certificate expiration date. It makes reusing the SDA data from another card harder and from an expired card impossible.

An example of Iissuer Public Key recovery can be found at *Section C.1 Issuer Certificate Generation and Public Key Recovery*.

Field Name	Length	Description
Start sentinel ("recovered data header")	1	0x6A
Certificate Format	1	0x02
Issuer Identifier	4	Leftmost 3 to 8 digits from the PAN (issuer BIN), padded with 0xF if needed
Certificate Expiration Date	2	Expiration date in MMYY binary-packed decimal format
Certificate Serial Number	3	A binary number assigned by the issuer and at issuer's discretion
Hash Algorithm Indicator	1	Identifies the hash algorithm. Currently only SHA-1 is supported, corresponding to the value of 0x01
Issuer Public Key Algorithm Indicator	1	Identifies the algorithm to be used with the issuer public key. Currently only RSA is supported, corresponding to the value of 0x01
Issuer Public Key Length	1	Length of the issuer public key modulus in bytes
Issuer Public Key Exponent Length	1	Length of the issuer public key exponent in bytes. Since only two public exponent values are supported, can only assume values of 1 or 3
Issuer Public Key or Leftmost Digits of the Issuer Public Key	212	Defined as the maximum CA length minus 36. Maximum CA length is 248. However, due to other protocol restrictions, the maximum length of an issuer public key is 247 bytes. Therefore, in case the issuer public key is of 212 bytes or more, up to 247, the 212 leftmost digits will be contained in this field. Alternatively, full issuer public key will be contained here, padded with the value of 0xBB to the full length of the field
Hash Result	20	Hash function output
End sentinel ("Recovered Data Trailer")	1	0xBC

Figure 3.1: Issuer key recovery header.

3.4.1.3 Authenticating the static data

For the static data authentication, the terminal needs to compare an independently calculated hash of card data to the one present on the card. To retrieve the latter, the Signed Static Application Data element, which was earlier retrieved from the card, is decrypted using the Issuer Public Key and the Issuer Public Key Exponent.

The decrypted data should contain the same sentinel values, 0x6A at the beginning and 0xBC at the end of the plaintext. The data has a header, a padding pattern of 0xBB values, and the 20-byte hash value immediately preceding the end sentinel.

The terminal must now prepare the input to the hash function to complete the static authentication. The input contains the values from the recovered header and the padding. To it, the terminal must append additional data from the card.

The process is as follows.

Immediately after the terminal selects an application, it issues the GET PROCESSING OPTIONS command, which returns, among other fields, the *application file locator (AFL)* and the *application interchange profile (AIP)*. The AFL instructs the terminal which files to request from the card application and the range of records to retrieve from these files. The AFL also indicates, for each file, how many records from the first record will be participating in the static authentication.

Depending on the file number, there are some differences in whether the records should be used as-is or a header tag should be stripped from them. Furthermore, the card can ask to include the AIP in the data authentication.

The terminal compiles the values in the order retrieved and appends them to the header. Then, an SHA-1 hash, H', is calculated using the accrued data as the input. The result must be identical to the provided value, H.

An example of static data authentication can be found at *Section C.2 Static Data Authentication and AFL*.

3.4.2 Dynamic data authentication

3.4.2.1 ICC key recovery

The dynamic data authentication (DDA) is possible if the card can perform RSA computations. In that case, the card stores, in addition to the issuer public key (signed by the CA private key), an individual key pair of the card called the ICC key.

The private key of the ICC key pair is stored on the card as-is since the card is using it to encrypt data during the interaction with the terminal. The public key is stored similarly to the issuer public key: with an ICC Public Key Certificate, an exponent value, and an optional ICC Public Key Remainder.

The issuer public key recovery process is identical to the case of static data authentication. The public key exponent is decrypted using the CA certificate, then the remainder, if present, is appended to it, and the hash value of the key is validated (see above, *Section 3.4.1.2 Key recovery*).

The terminal then performs another round of key recovery, using the issuer public key to decrypt the ICC Public Key Exponent and validating the hash value as described above.

The validation of the ICC key hash differs from that of the issuer key hash. Besides a different header, the validation of the ICC key hash includes static data authentication.

While during the validation of the issuer key, the hash included only the identifier of the issuer, with the ICC key, the hash includes the full PAN value. This difference is sensible: while for the issuer key, it was essential to ensure it belongs to the correct issuer, with the ICC key, we need to ascertain it belongs

Field Name	Length	Description
Start sentinel ("recovered data header")	1	0x6A
Certificate Format	1	0x04
Application PAN	10	The PAN, padded with 0xF to the full length of the field
Certificate Expiration Date	2	Expiration date in MMYY binary-packed decimal format
Certificate Serial Number	3	A binary number assigned by the issuer and at issuer's discretion
Hash Algorithm Indicator	1	Identifies the hash algorithm. Currently only SHA-1 is supported, corresponding to the value of 0x01
ICC Public Key Algorithm Indicator	1	Identifies the algorithm to be used with the ICC public key. Currently only RSA is supported, corresponding to the value of 0x01
ICC Public Key Length	1	Length of the ICC public key modulus in bytes
ICC Public Key Exponent Length	1	Length of the ICC public key exponent in bytes. Since only two public exponent values are supported, can only assume values of 1 or 3
ICC Public Key or Leftmost Digits of the ICC Public Key	$N_I - 36$	Here N_I is the length of the issuer key. The full ICC public key length depends on the protocol implementation, since the certificate cannot be longer than the key and must fit into an EMV protocol message at the same time. This puts the practical length if the ICC public key in the range between 205 and 240 bytes.
Hash Result	20	Hash function output
End sentinel ("Recovered Data Trailer")	1	0xBC

Figure 3.2: ICC key recovery header.

to the correct card. Hence, the terminal must compare the PAN that it has recovered from the ICC Public Key Certificate value to the one it obtained via other commands from the card application.

The input value for the ICC key validation hash also includes the static authentication data, gathered precisely in the same way as described in *Section 3.4.1 Static data authentication*. See also Figure 3.2 for details on the ICC key recovery header.

An example of ICC key recovery can be found in *C.3 ICC Certificate Generation and Public Key Recovery*.

3.4.2.2 Dynamic signature generation

Once the ICC public key has been recovered, the dynamic data authentication step is possible. As part of this process, the terminal gathers transaction-specific

Field Name	Length	Description
Start sentinel ("recovered data header")	1	0x6A
Signed Data Format	1	0x05
Hash Algorithm Indicator	1	Identifies the hash algorithm. Currently only SHA-1 is supported, corresponding to the value of 0x01
ICC Dynamic Data Length	1	Length of the ICC dynamic data in bytes
ICC Dynamic Data	L_{DD}	Dynamic data from the ICC
Pad Pattern	$N_{IC} - L_{DD} - 25$	Padding with 0xBB, where N_{IC} denotes the length of the ICC public key
Hash Result	20	Hash function output
End sentinel ("Recovered Data Trailer")	1	0xBC

Figure 3.3: Dynamic signature data.

data and an "unpredictable" number and sends it to the card as part of a dedicated command[2].

The mechanism that defines the exact values is called the *dynamic data object list (DDOL)*. The list will contain the tags and the lengths of the values the card requires for the dynamic data authentication. If there is no DDOL on the card, the terminal must have a default DDOL defined by the payment scheme in question. If the card's DDOL does not contain the unpredictable number value, the DDA is considered failed.

If there is a suitable DDOL either on the card or the terminal, the latter sends the command to the card, concatenating values in accordance with the DDOL.

The card generates a dynamic data value, either random or a counter, and concatenates the header fields, the dynamic data value, the padding, and the original data as provided by the terminal. The card then calculates the hash of the data (see Figure 3.3).

To sign the data with the ICC key, the card concatenates the sentinel value 0x6A with format indicators, appends the dynamic data that it has used as part of the hash input, adds padding, the hash result, and the data trailer 0xBC, then encrypts the resulting sequence with its private key. The ciphertext, the firsttermdynamic signature, is sent to the terminal in the command response.

The terminal uses the recovered ICC public key to decrypt the response. The terminal knew all the hash function inputs except the card's dynamic data. The card provides this value separately, and the terminal can access it by decrypting the dynamic signature value. Once the terminal has obtained this value, it can calculate and validate the hash.

An example of Dynamic Signature Generation can be found at *Section C.4 Dynamic Signature Generation*.

---

[2]INTERNAL AUTHENTICATE [53]

3.4.2.3   Combined data authentication

The combined data authentication shortens the message exchange between the terminal and the card while retaining the security benefits of the dynamic data authentication process.

The key recovery steps of the CDA are identical to those of the dynamic data authentication. The terminal recovers the issuer public key and then the ICC public key, performing static data authentication in the process.

As part of the EMV flow, the terminal can issue one or two requests to generate an application cryptogram (GENERATE AC) to the card. The terminal can request CDA by setting a bit in the request command. If the flow only has one cryptogram generation request, the CDA is performed with it. Otherwise, the CDA is performed with the second cryptogram request.

While with the dedicated command, either the card or the terminal must maintain a separate DOL, a DOL is already present with the cryptogram command.

Therefore, for the combined data authentication, the card concatenates a dynamic value, any input parameters it has received with the command, and the output it has returned. The terminal then follows the process described in *Section 3.4.2 Dynamic data authentication* to validate the signature.

3.4.3   Cardholder verification

The EMV technology allows a variety of cardholder verification methods. While formerly the primary method to verify the cardholder identity was to compare signatures, the ICC enabled several methods to verify the PIN instead. With the contactless protocols, the standard was later enhanced to allow the new *consumer device cardholder verification method* (*CDCVM*), where the device used in place of the payment card performs a form of cardholder authentication (such as entering the device PIN or using a biometric method to validate identity).

The range of supported cardholder verification methods [3]includes cardholder signature, several types of PINs, the CDCVM, and a "no CVM" method. The latter may be used for small tickets such as at a vending machine or in cases such as the public transit, where an additional verification will cause massive passenger congestion.

The terminal may not support all of these methods: for example, a terminal may not have a PIN pad or a printer for the signature slip. The card contains CVM rules, including use cases and amount limits. The terminal processes the list of rules while considering its own settings, and the two parties agree on a CVM to be used.

---

[3]For the full list, see for example Section 5.3.10 in [47] or Section 10.5 in [54].

Figure 3.4: Format 2 PIN block.

Methods such as signature, no CVM, or CDCVM involve no cryptography and are therefore not in the scope of this book. Cryptography is involved with methods that validate the PIN value.

The PIN can be validated either by the card or by the issuer. In the former case, the validation is called *offline PIN*; in the latter, *online PIN*. The offline PIN, in turn, can be validated either as plaintext or as ciphertext.

3.4.3.1 PIN block format 2 and offline plaintext validation

While plaintext validation, obviously, does not require any cryptography, the format of the PIN block is shared. The ISO 9564 standard defines several PIN block formats [56], also found in the "Acquiring Card Payments," Chapter 13 [47]. The interaction between the terminal and the card is based on the Format 2 PIN block, which is as follows (see Figure 3.4).

The PIN block is an 8-byte packed BCD array. Its first nibble contains the format code, 2, the second nibble specifies the PIN length L (4 till 13, as a hexadecimal digit), followed by PIN digits P and padded with 0xF to the full length of the block.

If the supported and the chosen CVM is plaintext offline PIN, the terminal sends the PIN block to the card as-is, and the card validates the PIN value.

3.4.3.2 Encrypted offline PIN

The encrypted PIN validation flow puts demand on the card's resources. As the name implies, the terminal encrypts the PIN block and sends it to the card while enciphered.

The PIN block is encrypted with an RSA public key. An *encrypted PIN block* is also referred to as the *EPB*. The card may contain a dedicated PIN Encipherment Public Key, which is recovered in the same manner as the ICC Public Key that is used for the DDA/CDA (see *Section 3.4.2.1 ICC key recovery*). If the card does not contain a dedicated ICC PIN Encipherment Key, the ICC Public Key is used instead.

In order to perform the validation, the terminal first requests a challenge from the card. A challenge is an 8-byte unpredictable number that the card returns in response to a dedicated command, GET CHALLENGE.

After receiving the number, the terminal forms the enciphered PIN block by concatenating a data header of 0x7F, the PIN block, and the unpredictable number. The terminal then adds random padding to the length of the key (either the Pin Encipherment Public Key or the ICC Public Key), encrypts the result, and sends it to the card for verification.

The card, in its turn, deciphers the input, checks the header value, and then confirms that the unpredictable number is the one formerly provided in response to the GET CHALLENGE command.

3.4.3.3   Online PIN

Unlike the offline PIN, where the card is actively participating in the cardholder verification, selecting the online PIN as the CVM means that the issuer will perform the verification. In other words, the card negotiates the use of the method, leaving its actual execution to the terminal.

The EMV standard does not govern the implementation of the capturing of the PIN for the online validation. Instead, the payment card industry sets security requirements for the device and the overall processing solution in the PCI PTS and the PCI PIN standards (see *Sections 6.2.1 PCI PIN standard* and *6.2.2 PCI PIN Transaction Security standard (PTS), SPoC, and CPoC*).

Since these standards aim to define security requirements for any interaction with the cardholder PIN, they prescribe compliance with the EMV standard for offline PIN authentication and alignment with the requirements of ISO 9564 for PIN handling in general [56].

From this set of standards, it follows that a compliant terminal can use Format 0, Format 3, or Format 4 PIN blocks for the online PIN transmission. Furthermore, the list of permitted algorithms for encryption of the PIN block contains RSA (used for encrypted offline PIN, see *Section 3.4.3.2 Encrypted offline PIN*), TDES, and AES only.

3.4.3.4   PIN block formats 0, 1, 3, and 4

According to the ISO 9564 standard [56], PIN Block Format 2 (see *Section 3.4.3.1 PIN block format 2 and offline plaintext validation*) is allowed only for local use with offline systems. For the online PIN transmission, other PIN block formats must be used.

The format depends on the algorithm used for the PIN encryption since the lengths of these formats differ. PIN Block Formats 0 and 3 have the length of 8 bytes, while Format 4 has the length of 16 bytes. The symmetric algorithms recommended for these formats are TDES and AES, correspondingly.

Formats 0 and 3 are a product of a XOR of two 8-byte blocks.

The first block contains a nibble with the format indicator (0 or 3), a nibble with the PIN length, and the PIN digits. Format 0 and format 3 define different paddings of the block: while with format 0, the vector is padded with the value of 0xF, with format 3, the padding (denoted by R) is random. See also Figure 3.5.

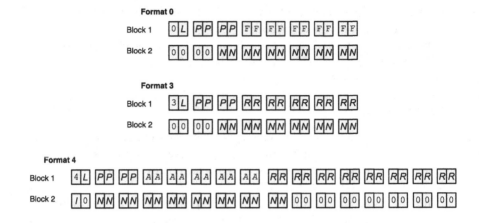

Figure 3.5: PIN block formats 0, 3, and 4.

The second block is the same in both formats and contains 12 right-most digits of the PAN (denoted by N in the figure), excluding the check digit, left-padded with zeroes.

Format 4 is an extension and improvement of Formats 0 and 3, which enlarges the block size to 16 bytes, suitable for the AES algorithm. Format 4 also uses two 16-byte blocks, but instead of XOR-ing them together prior to encryption, they are encrypted in the CBC mode (see *Section 1.8.1 Padding and cipher block chaining*), i.e., the first block is encrypted, XOR-ed with the second block, and the result is encrypted again.

The first block of Format 4 is similar to the first block of Format 0, except that the value of 0xA is used for padding instead of 0xF. The vector is further padded with 8 more random bytes.

The second block contains the PAN without the check digit, padded with zero. The first nibble of the second block indicates the PAN length l without the check digit and minus 12. That is, if the PAN has 14 digits, the length nibble is $14 - 1 - 12 = 1$, where the extra -1 accounts for the check digit.

The PIN Block Format 1 is intended for use when no PAN data is available. It is formed by concatenating a single nibble indicator of the format, 0x1, with the PIN length in nibbles, followed by the PIN value and padded to the full length of the block with either a random value or some unique transaction identifier.

3.4.3.5 Key management methods

As mentioned above, the only permitted algorithms for PIN encryption are RSA, TDES, and AES. The speed of the symmetric algorithms makes them the preferable choice for implementations. Furthermore, all major card schemes expect to receive the PIN block under a symmetric algorithm, and, therefore, the use of RSA for the online PIN encryption, while theoretically possible, is rare if not nonexistent.

Therefore, point-of-sale devices, terminals, acquirers, schemes, and issuers need key management schemes or processes to ensure the keys' secure conveyance for these algorithms.

A direct approach would be to store unique keys per each issuer or acquirer and each terminal, which is clearly not feasible. Two principles were adopted to simplify the task.

First, the chain of hosts which participates in a transaction flow is divided into zones, with a translation of encrypted data from one key to another happening within hosts on zone boundaries.

Second, since the cards and terminals operate in an environment far less secure than the host, the system should resist a mass compromise: keys stolen from a single POS should not endanger all other POS devices.

However, storing individual keys per card or terminal would create a considerable overhead for the corresponding hosts. Hence, in these scenarios, the preferred key management mechanism is to have each card or terminal possess an individual key, while the acquirer or the issuer host can easily derive it from a securely stored master value.

Methods for managing keys between hosts are described in *Section 5.2 Zoning*.

There are two popular methods for the segment between the terminal and the terminal management system: the Master/Session protocol and the DUKPT algorithm.

With the Master/Session protocol, a master key is securely preloaded into the POS devices. The host generates and communicates a session key, encrypted with the master key, to the terminal during device operation. Since the device already has the preinstalled master key, ut can decrypt the session key and then use it to encrypt PIN blocks.

The *Derived Unique Key Per Transaction* (*DUKPT*) protocol allows generating an individual key per transaction on the POS device based on an initial preloaded key. The host can independently generate the same key value, thus establishing the mutually shared key for the symmetric encryption algorithm. The protocol is described in *Section 5.4 Derived Unique Key Per Transaction* (*DUKPT*).

3.4.4 *Application cryptograms and issuer authentication*

After the terminal has performed a series of checks and has authenticated the card, it negotiates the CVM and possibly executes it. At this point, the terminal can decide on the fate of the transaction itself.

A terminal can make three possible decisions: approve the transaction offline, request an online issuer confirmation, and decline the transaction. The card confirms the decision by generating a cryptogram. Three cryptogram types correspond to the three possible decisions: the *Transaction Certificate* (*TC*) for an approved transaction, the *Authorization Request Cryptogram* (*ARQC*), and the *Application Authentication Cryptogram* (*AAC*).

The terminal suggests its decision to the card, which can then either agree and cooperate with the terminal or lower the level of the cryptogram it will generate. The priority of the cryptograms is TC, ARQC, and AAC. Correspondingly, the card can always agree to the terminal's suggestion, decline the transaction with an AAC, or respond with an ARQC to the request of the TC.

The ARQC is sent to the issuer alongside standard transaction details. The issuer provides an *Authorization Response Cryptogram* (*ARPC*) and, possibly, some commands for the card to execute.

Since, in the case of contact transactions, the time for the interaction with the card is unlimited, the protocol allows waiting for the issuer's response to arrive and be sent to the card for an additional issuer authentication, thus ensuring the response indeed came from a valid issuer. Most implementations do not support this step with contactless transactions due to the lack of time.

For the cryptogram, the EMV standard does not mandate a specific implementation of the ARQC, allowing each scheme or even issuer to devise a scheme of their own. However, the standard implementation is widely used with minor changes in practice.

The recommended approach for the symmetric key used to generate cryptograms is to create a master key on the issuer side and store it securely, then use it to derive the ICC Master Keys per each card. During the interaction with the terminal, the card can generate a one-time Session key which will be used for the cryptogram itself.

3.4.4.1 Master key derivation

The idea behind the master key derivation is that each card would get a unique master key which is hard to guess, while the issuer host would store a very limited number of keys but, given the PAN and the CSN, would be able to reconstruct the unique key quickly.

The issuer generates an *issuer master key* (*IMK*), either a double-length TDES key or an AES key. Further steps depend on the algorithm chosen. Other names for this key include *master derivation key* (*MDK*), *derivation master key* (*DMK*), *derivation master key for authentication cryptograms* (*DMK-AC*), and *master key for authentication cryptograms* (*MK-AC*).

The issuer derives the *ICC master key* (*ICC MK*) from the issuer master key. It is also known as the *derived key for authentication cryptograms* (*DK-AC*).

For the TDES encryption, the standard provides two options. The options, named *Option A* and *Option B*, generate the base of the input for the TDES algorithm, denoted as Y.

Option A applies when the application PAN is equal to or less than 16 digits long. The steps are as follows:

1. The sequence number (CSN) is appended to the PAN.

2. The result is right-padded with zeros if its length is less than 8 bytes.

3. The rightmost 8 bytes of the result is the sought Y.

Option B applies when the application PAN is longer than 16 digits. The steps of option B are as follows:

1. The CSN is appended to the PAN. If no CSN is available, two zeroes are appended instead. If the total number of nibbles is odd, the value is left padded with a single zero.

2. The result is hashed using SHA-1.

3. The result of the hash, in turn, is decimalized (see *Section A.7 Decimalization*) to obtain 16 decimal digits.

4. The output of the decimalization is the value Y.

Once Y is available, it can be used to calculate the ICC master key. The left and the right halves of the ICC master key are calculated separately:

1. The value of Y is encrypted with TDES using the issuer master key to obtain the left half of the key.

2. The value of Y is negated by applying either bitwise NOT or XOR with the mask of 0xFF.

3. The outcome of Step 2 is encrypted with TDES using the issuer master key to obtain the right half of the key.

4. The left and the right halves are concatenated, and parity bits are corrected in the outcome to form a valid TDES key.

The method for master key derivation with AES (also called Option C) is as follows:

1. The PAN and the CSN are concatenated and right padded with zeros to the length of 16 bytes to obtain Y.

2. Y is encrypted with AES using the issuer master key.

3. If the desired key length is greater than 128 bit, Y is negated to obtain Y': $Y' = \sim Y$.

4. Y' is encrypted with AES using the issuer master key.

5. Depending on the desired key length, either 64 or 128 bits of encrypted Y' are appended to the encrypted Y to obtain the AES key of the desired length.

Examples of ICC key derivation can be found in *C.5 ICC Master Key Derivation*.

3.4.4.2 Session key derivation

The session key derivation process is provided as a recommendation by the EMV standard but is widely adopted. The process introduces a diversification value to the ICC master key that differs per transaction. The key is also called the *application cryptogram session key (SKAC)*.

The EMV application specification [54] defines an *application transaction counter (ATC)*, a 2-byte counter value that the card increases with each transaction. This value serves as a basis for value diversification.

The process is almost identical for TDES and AES and varies slightly only depending on the desired output length of the key. The output length can either be the same as the block size of the algorithm (64 bits for DES and 128 for AES) or larger (for example, the session key might be 128 bits for DES or 192 or 256 bits for AES), the "short" and the "long" version, correspondingly.

For the short version, the algorithm steps are as follows:

1. The card pads the ATC value (two bytes) with zeroes to the length of the input block.

2. The card then encrypts the resulting value with the ICC master key using the symmetric algorithm of choice.

3. If the algorithm for the ARQC is DES, the less significant bit of each byte of the key is modified to ensure odd bit parity.

For the long version, the card runs the encryption algorithm twice:

1. The card appends the value of 0xF0 to the ATC value and zero-pads the result to the full length of the input block.

2. The card encrypts the result to obtain the first part of the session key.

3. Next, the card appends the value of 0x0F to the ATC and zero-pads the result to the full length of the input block.

4. The card encrypts the result to obtain the second part of the session key.

5. The two outputs are concatenated. If the desired key is an AES-192 key, the output is truncated to 192 bits. If the desired key is a TDES key, the parity bit of each byte is adjusted.

An example of session key derivation can be found in *Section 3.4.4.2 Session key derivation.*

3.4.4.3   Generation of the cryptogram

Once the session key is derived, the card can generate the requested cryptogram. The cryptogram is a MAC of some transaction data, both data elements that were sent from the terminal and those stored by the card.

The specific list of data elements depends on a particular implementation. The EMV standard recommends a minimum set of values but does not mandate it.

The exact length of the data can vary. The ARQC, as defined in the standard [53], is a MAC of the data (see *Section 1.9 Message Authentication Codes*). The algorithm for TDES encryption with a double-length key is as follows:

1. The value of 0x80 is appended to the data.

2. The result is padded so that its length is a multiple of 8 bytes and is split into 8-byte chunks.

3. The key is split into two halves, K_1 and K_2.

4. The data is encrypted with the single DES algorithm in the CBC mode (see *Section 1.8.1 Padding and cipher block chaining*) using the session key's first half and a zero initialization vector. In other words, for each chunk, the output of the previous round is XORed with the chunk and then fed into the next round.

5. The result is decrypted using the second half of the session key.

6. The result is encrypted again using the first half of the session key.

7. The outcome is the ARQC.

In other words, rather than chaining Triple DES encryption in the CBC mode, the algorithm chains single DES encryption with the first half of the key and performs a single TDES encryption on its last iteration.

An example of ARQC generation can be found in *C.7 ARQC Generation.*

3.4.4.4   Issuer authentication

With a contact EMV transaction, the card stays connected to the terminal long enough to process the response from the issuer. It helps authenticate the issuer, confirming that the responder to the transaction request is the entity that is authorized to do so.

The authentication response cryptogram, ARPC, is received from the issuer and passed to the card for that purpose.

Before generating the response cryptogram, the issuer decides on the transaction's *authorization response code (ARC)*. It is primarily a business/risk decision, although the issuer can reject the transaction due to failed online PIN verification or other authentication error. The ARC is a two-byte field.

The EMV standard recommends two alternatives for issuer authentication. Method 1 generates an 8-byte ARPC value. With this method, the issuer performs the following actions:

1. The card's ICC master key is derived from the issuer master key.

2. The card's session key is derived from the ICC master key.

3. The ARC is right-padded with zeroes to the required block size (depending on the algorithm used), and the ARQC, as received, is XORed with the padded ARC. It is the same as XORing the first two bytes of the ARQC with the ARC.

4. The outcome is encrypted using TDES or AES with the previously recovered session key.

5. The output of the encryption is the ARPC value.

This method allows the card to confirm that the issuer has indeed responded while also digitally signing the authorization response code. While performing the reverse actions to confirm the ARPC, the card will only obtain the original ARQC value if the independently provided ARC is identical to the one used by the issuer. Therefore, an attacker cannot modify that cleartext field to make a decline transaction appear approved.

Method 2 generates a 4-byte ARPC value. The issuer can return additional or more elaborate response elements to the card. One such element is called the *card status update (CSU)*, and it is of 4-byte length. In addition to it, the issuer may return up to 8 bytes of *proprietary authentication data* to the card. To calculate the ARPC, the issuer performs the following actions:

1. The card's ICC master key is derived from the issuer master key.

2. The card's session key is derived from the ICC master key.

3. The ARQC, as received, is concatenated with the CSU, and the proprietary authentication data.

4. The signature of the resulting value is generated using the same method as with the ARQC (see *Section 3.4.4.3 Generation of the cryptogram*).

5. Four leading bytes of the signature are concatenated with the CSU and the proprietary authentication data.

6. The output is the ARPC value.

An example of the ARPC generation can be found in *Section C.8 ARPC Generation.*

Chapter 4

Securing the Network

Unlike other topics this book covers, network security is not specific to payments. However, it is an essential component at the backbone of any payment solution and, therefore, must be well understood by a payments professional.

Two protocol families are particularly relevant to the field of payments. One is the *Transport Layer Security* (*TLS*), formerly known as the *secure sockets layer* (*SSL*); the other is the *JSON Web Encryption, JSON Web Signature, JSON Web Algorithms, JSON Web Key*, and more (*JWE, JWS, JWA*, and *JWK*, accordingly), jointly known as *JSON Object Signing and Encryption* (*JOSE*).

The TLS protocol is used practically everywhere. It is a standard, convenient and secure way to safeguard the transmission of sensitive data in a manner that is nearly transparent to many payment applications. The design goals of the protocol were to achieve confidentiality, authentication, and integrity over a network that is entirely under the control of an attacker.

The JOSE family of protocols provides JSON-based structures for communicating encrypted or signed data in the JSON format. Adherence to this format considerably simplifies the development of security features in internet and mobile applications, allowing for another layer of application-level security. These protocols are, for example, used in the EMV 3D-S Secure authentication protocol to secure the mobile SDK.

In addition to these network layer protocols, the chapter contains the description of the EMV 3-D Secure protocol, which was designed purposefully to authenticate online card payments.

DOI: 10.1201/9781003371366-4

4.1 Transport Layer Security (TLS)

One of this protocol's first and relatively weak implementations was "Secure Sockets Layer" or SSL. The Transport Layer Security (TLS) protocol has long supplanted SSL, but the name is still in use.

The TLS protocol is a hybrid method that combines asymmetric handshake and the establishment of keys with symmetric encryption of the data exchange.

Unlike more specific schemes such as the ECIES, the TLS protocol does not prescribe a specific method for any of its steps. Instead, the client provides a list of acceptable and supported (see Figure 4.1) algorithms, from which the server chooses the preferable one(s).

The protocol has a handshake step, and the data transmission can commence upon a successful handshake.

The server can accept any client or insist on authentication of client certificates. The opposite is not true: the client always authenticates the server.

The handshake step has three major phases:

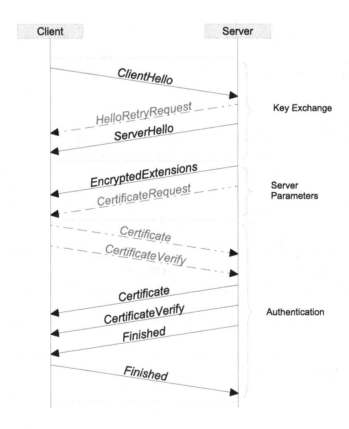

Figure 4.1: TLS protocol handshake.

1. Key Exchange – during this phase, the parties agree on a key exchange method and choose cipher options.

2. Server Parameters – during this phase, other handshake parameters are established (for example, whether client authentication is required).

3. Authentication – the client authenticates the server and vice versa. The server can request to delay the client authentication to a later stage in the data exchange.

4.1.1 Extensions

Besides the basic protocol, TLS allows for multiple protocol extensions. IANA maintains the official registry of standard extensions, while private-use extensions are also allowed [57].

The extensions are part of a fixed field in the protocol messages. Instead, they are sent in the tag-length-value format. Despite the name, some extensions must be present to establish the session successfully.

For example, if the server supports multiple virtual hosts, the client can specify during the handshake which specific host it is willing to access. The client can do so by using the standard extension `server_name`.

Another example is the cryptographic negotiation. Let us assume that the client has indicated that it wishes to exchange keys using the elliptic curve Diffie-Helman method. The client can further specify the particular elliptic curves it supports through the `supported_groups` extension.

The client and the server use the `supported_versions` extension to indicate TLS versions they are willing to support in this session.

The parties also exchange a list of supported CAs via the `certificate_authorities` extension. The CAs are provided as X.501 distinguished names [58].

While there are many very well-built implementations of the protocol in libraries and network appliances, it has many options and parameters, a high-level understanding of which can help troubleshoot a system or enhance its security.

4.1.2 Key exchange

During the key exchange, the client sends to the server a *ClientHello* message. The message has the following content:

1. The list of encryption algorithms that the client supports. The list includes AEAD algorithms for encryption and signing of the messages (see *Section 1.9.5 Authenticated encryption*) and an HMAC key derivation function (see *Section 1.10 Randomness and Key Derivation*).

2. The list of supported algorithms for establishing the mutual secret key (e.g., Diffie-Hellman) in the `supported_groups` extension. The client

can also offer public values for some of the supported algorithms to the server. E.g., if the protocol is Diffie-Hellman, the client can send $A \equiv g^a mod p$ in the key_share extension. Alternatively, the client can send nothing, in which case the server will respond with a list of supported algorithms, but then another handshake roundtrip will be required.

3. As part of the later Authentication stage, the server and the client sign the messages they send. Furthermore, the certificates which are validated during the Authentication stage are also signed using some signature algorithms. Both are independent of the signature method used in the AEAD scheme. Hence, the message contains a signature_algorithms and a signature_algorithms_cert extensions to specify the methods that will be used for these purposes.

4. It is possible to pre-share keys for the data encryption via some secure external channel. Such a *pre-shared key* (*PSK*) can be used to encrypt the application data or as a basis to generate a new session key (thus protecting new sessions from a possible compromise of an old key). These two options are provided via pre_shared_key and psk_key_exchange_modes extensions, accordingly. Furthermore, TLS uses the PSK facility to resume a previously established session.

Upon receiving the ClientHello message, the server responds with a *Server-Hello* or a *HelloRetryRequest*.

The HelloRetryRequest message means that the server would like the client to retry and provide more details with its next ClientHello session. For example, as mentioned above, if the client did not provide the first value of the final field DH protocol, but the protocol itself is acceptable to both parties, the server will use the HelloRetryRequest message to request that the client would share the value of A.

The server would send the ServerHello message if it could select the necessary cryptographic methods and find a set of handshake parameters that is sufficient and acceptable to proceed. The message can only include a single cipher method.

Both the client and the server include a random number in their respective Hello messages. This measure helps prevent replay attacks.

4.1.3 Server parameters

At this stage of the handshake, the server has enough information to derive all the keys it will need for the data exchange.

For instance, with the finite field Diffie-Hellman, the server has already received the public parameters from the client and can derive the shared secret. Since it has already chosen the cipher suite, it can derive the actual encryption key.

At this point, the server sends the mandatory *EncryptedExtensions* message, which contains all extensions that are not required to set up cryptography and can therefore be encrypted. The client must validate these extensions, at least checking the list for any invalid ones (and, on the way, ensuring that the traffic encryption is ready to go).

After the mandatory EncryptedExtensions message, the server can send the optional *CertificateRequest* message. This message can either contain details regarding the certificate that the server would like to see right now or indicate that the certificate will be requested from the client at a later stage during the data exchange. If the parties work with a pre-shared key, the server cannot require an immediate certificate from the client since a pre-shared key is considered sufficient to establish the session. However, the server can still ask for a client certificate at a later stage. The act of requesting the certificate after the handshake is called *post-handshake authentication.*

4.1.4   Authentication

The authentication phase of the handshake consists of three messages, *Certificate*, *CertificateVerify*, and *Finished*.

Besides the message-specific data, each message contains an HMAC of all previous messages of the ongoing handshake.

The Certificate message communicates the certificate chain of the party that sends it. The CertificateVerify message contains proof that the sending party indeed possesses the private key of the certificate. Finished indicates that the party has completed its side of the handshake, has received and validated all messages from the counterpart, and is ready to exchange data once it receives and validates the Finished message from the other party.

The server always sends the Certificate and the CertificateVerify messages to the client, followed by the Finished message.

The client sends its Certificate and CertificateVerify only if requested by the server. If the server did not ask for the client's certificates, it sends the Finished message only.

4.1.5   Implementation considerations

There are several significant considerations for TLS use in a solution.

Selecting the cipher suite and the protocol version is usually easy – there always is an applicable industry or regulatory standard that describes the minimum key length, approved hash functions, approved encryption algorithms, et cetera.

Most concerns with a TLS solution design revolve around certificate management and depend on many factors, including the target audience of the solution.

An important rule a solution with TLS involved is to set up a mechanism to remind the operational personnel about upcoming expiry dates of certificates.

Many a good processing company had experienced downtime because of a certificate that was not updated on time.

It is also prudent to check that the platform chosen supports the necessary certification management options at an early step during the design phase[1].

Server-side authentication considerations depend on the client base.

For the broadest possible user base, the server must always have the updated certificate corresponding to its domain, signed by a large and trusted CA. All browsers ship with a list of preinstalled CA root certificates. Hence, the CA for the server certificate should be chosen among those available on every recent browser.

If the users can actually be expected to perform some custom steps on their machines, or when the user endpoints are managed centrally, the server may be configured to request a valid client certificate. In that case, dedicated certificates must be installed and later managed on the client-side. On the server side, the relevant CA root certificate (if using a proprietary CA) must be deployed and the necessary configuration changes made to ensure the CertificateRequest will be sent to the client during the handshake.

With the implementation of the PSD2 access to account API, the payment service providers (the API consumers) are issued test and live certificates by about a dozen special-purpose CAs in Europe. The banks (which provide the APIs) were to allow any consumer with a valid certificate to connect to the API. However, only the designated CAs were to be supported. During the implementation, this required replacing the standard certificate store with a completely custom one and also impacted platform patching and system maintenance.

If the use of the SSL is purely internal, the certificates can be self-signed. In that case, the signing entity and the user entity for such a certificate are the same. However, the self-signed certificates carry no trust value, and setting up a custom CA is advised instead.

Another security aspect that is often overlooked is the certificate revocation. It differs from expiry in that the revocation happens due to a security incident or another event that is external to the certificate infrastructure.

As mentioned in *Section 1.11 Key Trust and Key Certificates*, there are two methods to track revoked certificates: the certificate revocation lists (CRLs) and the online requests via the online certificate status (OCSP) protocol. The solution should support at least one or possibly both of these methods, depending on the constraints.

If the solution has an online connection and the user experience can tolerate a roundtrip to an OCSP server, its use is preferable. Alternatively, if the solution is walled in or time-sensitive, a custom CRL and a process to keep it up to date might be a good idea.

An example of a TLS client is found in *Section B.10 TLS Client*.

---

[1] The author had encountered a situation when a standard cloud-based TLS component did not support the *removal* of root CAs which was mandatory for a compliant solution.

4.2 JSON Object Signing and Encryption (JOSE)

The JSON Object Signing and Encryption (JOSE) is a set of standards for representing encrypted and signed content using JSON-based data structures. There are no explicit cryptographic methods or algorithms which are part of the standard family. Instead, it provides a method to represent and serialize data like signatures, encryption keys, algorithms used, et cetera, in the JSON format [59].

The JOSE standards include:

- JSON Web Encryption (JWE) standard, which defines the representation of encrypted content [60].

- JSON Web Signature (JWS) standard, which defines the representation of digital signatures and MACs [61].

- JSON Web Algorithms (JWA) standard, which defines the cryptographic algorithms and identifiers for use with JWE [62].

- JSON Web Key (JWK) standard, which represents a set of keys [63].

JWE, JWS, JWA, and JWK will be required to represent an encrypted and signed message.

The JWE and JWS standards define several types of serialization: compact, JSON, and flattened JSON. The JSON and flattened JSON serializations describe a JSON format that is not URL-safe, can contain whitespaces, and is not used in the protocols mentioned in this book. Therefore, only compact serialization will be described below in the relevant chapters.

4.2.1 *JSON web algorithms (JWA)*

The JSON Web Algorithms standard defines the names and identifiers for cryptographic algorithms for use with the JWK, JWS, and JWE specifications [62]. The JWA lists algorithms for digital signatures and MACs, key management, key agreement, key encryption, content encryption, and representation of public and private keys.

The JWA RFC provides details on some parameter values and refers to a public IANA registry that is kept up to date with a complete list of parameter values and cross-references to other RFCs which introduce and describe them. For example, support for Edwards curve cryptography (an alternative to elliptic curves) was introduced as a later RFC and can be discovered and reached via IANA [64] but not via the JWA RFC 7518.

Upon encountering a parameter for which the specified value is unclear, the best course is to consult the IANA registry first, then follow the links to the specific RFCs for details.

4.2.2 JSON web key (JWK)

A JWK represents a cryptographic key [63].

Each JWK object can have the following fields:

- kty, specifying the key type. It is a mandatory field that can have values RSA (for the RSA algorithm, see *Section 1.5.1 RSA*), EC (for elliptic curve cryptography, see *Section 1.6 Elliptic-Curve Cryptography (ECC)*), or oct for representation of symmetric keys.

- use, specifying the intended use of the key. It is an optional field with values sig (signature) and enc (encryption), which may have additional values. Alternatively, the key_ops field may be used instead.

- alg, specifying the algorithm to use with the key.

- kid, specifying the key ID. An optional field.

- x5u, x5c, x5t, x5t#S256 fields, containing a URL for an X.509 certificate, an X.509 certificate chain (in the form of an array), an X.509 certificate SHA-1 thumbprint, and an X.509 certificate SHA-256 thumbprint.

In addition, the JWK object must contain parameters for the specific key according to the JWA specification.

If the algorithm is RSA, the JWK object has two additional mandatory members, n and e, corresponding to the modulus and the exponent of the public RSA key. The values are base64 URL encodings of the actual value in the big-endian representation. In addition, the object can contain values of d (private exponent), p and q (first and second prime factor), and other information.

If the algorithm is EC, the JWK object has three additional mandatory members, crv, x, and y. The crv member specifies the cryptographic curve in use and can assume values P-256, P-384, P-521, another value from the corresponding IANA registry [65], or an implementation-specific curve name. The x and y values contain the corresponding coordinates of the elliptic curve point, represented as base64 URL encodings of the values in the big-endian representation. The value of d (ECC private key) can also be part of the JWK object.

4.2.3 JSON web signature (JWS)

The JSON Web Signature (JWS) represents either digitally signed content or for which a MAC was computed [60].

A JWS contains three parts: header, payload, and signature. The header can further contain protected and unprotected data. The former will be included while calculating the signature; the latter will not.

The header, also called the JOSE Header, can contain the following parameters:

- `alg` parameter, identifying the algorithm used for the signature. The value is according to JWA and the corresponding IANA registry (see *Section 4.2.1 JSON web algorithms (JWA)*) [64].

- `jku` parameter, containing a URL through which keys for signature validation can be retrieved.

- `jwk` parameter contains the public key corresponding to the key used to sign the JWS in the JWK format (see *Section 4.2.2 JSON web key (JWK)*).

- `kid` parameter, specifying the key ID.

- `x5u`, `x5c`, `x5t`, `x5t#S256` optional parameters, containing X.509 certificate details (see *Section 4.2.2 JSON web key (JWK)*).

- `typ` and `cty` parameters, identifying the content type, and `crit` parameter, identifying a protocol extension parameter critical for the receiving application to process.

The JWS Compact Serialization contains three base64-encoded strings, separated by a dot: the header, the payload, and the signature.

To calculate a basic JWS, first, the protected header must be composed. Assuming that no certificate needs to be checked and that the key and the content type are known to the recipient, the protected header only needs to contain the algorithm. Assuming that the header is Base64-encoded to V and the payload is Base64-encoded to P, the signature is obtained as $S = H(V \parallel . \parallel P)$. The result is Base64 encoded, and the full compact JSON representation of the JWS will be of the form $V \parallel . \parallel P \parallel . \parallel S$.

4.2.4   *JSON web encryption (JWE)*

The JSON Web Encryption (JWE) represents encrypted content. It utilizes authenticated encryption for the payload; therefore, a signature in the JWS format is not required if the JWE format is used.

The full specification of the JWE contains capabilities such as per-recipient communications. In payments, these are not in use due to the peer-to-peer nature of most protocols.

The JWE uses the notion of the *content encryption key* (*CEK*) for the key that's used to encrypt the payload.

A JWE object contains the following parts:

- JOSE Header.

- JWE Encrypted Key.

- JWE Initialization Vector.

■ JWE Additional Authenticated Data (AAD).

■ JWE Ciphertext.

■ JWE Authentication Tag.

The JOSE header contains protected and two unprotected parts, shared and per-recipient. The latter two are not in the scope of this section.

The header contains the following parameters:

■ alg, specifying the algorithm with which the CEK is encrypted or its value is otherwise determined. For instance, in the case of a key agreement scheme such as DHE or ECDHE, it will be specified in this field.

■ enc, specifying the algorithm with which the payload is encrypted. Only AEAD (see *Section 1.9.5 Authenticated encryption*) algorithms are allowed.

■ zip, specifying the optional compression algorithm that may be applied to the payload before encryption.

■ Other headers such as jku, jwk, kid, x5u, and related, as described in *Section 4.2.3 JSON web signature (JWS)*.

The standard allows several methods for CEK negotiation. The CEK can be encrypted with a public key or wrapped with a symmetric key. The CEK can be either generated as part of a key agreement algorithm (this method is called *Direct Key Agreement*) or, otherwise, the key agreement can yield the key with which a randomly generated CEK will be encrypted. Finally, the CEK can be pre-shared.

Only the Direct Key Agreement method is currently used for protocols in this book, and consequently, only it will be covered.

Assuming the Direct Key Agreement mode without additional authenticated data, the steps to encrypt and sign a message will be as follows:

1. Using the jku or jwk parameters, obtain keys for the key agreement algorithm.

2. Derive the CEK.

3. Generate a random initialization vector *IV* for the algorithm, if required.

4. Prepare the JOSE header *JH* for the message, specifying the alg, enc, and other necessary parameters.

5. Set the additional authenticated data to be the Base64-encoded *JH*.

6. Encrypt the payload using the *IV* and the additional authenticated data to obtain the ciphertext *C* and the authentication tag *T*.

7. Serialize the output as: $base64(JH) \parallel . \parallel . \parallel base64(IV) \parallel . \parallel base64(C) \parallel . \parallel base64(T)$. Note that the subsequent two dots after the JOSE header are because CEK is not being shared since it is being recovered using a key agreement mechanism.

4.3 3D Secure and EMV 3-D Secure

4.3.1 Introduction

While there are efficient means of encrypting the communications between the user's device and the payment gateway, cardholder authentication is challenging in the online world.

With a card, there are cryptographic means to authenticate the card itself (see *Section 3.4 Card authentication*) and means to verify the cardholder (see *Section 3.4.3 Cardholder verification*) by the card itself or via a request to the issuer bank.

Over the years, card schemes tried several approaches to improve online cardholder verification. The two mechanisms which were deployed and remained in use are the *address verification service* (*AVS*) and the CVV_2.

With the address verification service, the cardholder is prompted for the billing address. It is then forwarded to the card issuer alongside the rest of the transaction details, and the issuer verifies that the address matches the one on file.

With the CVV_2 method, the CVV generation algorithm of the magnetic stripe is reused for online payments. A CVV value is generated as described in *Section 3.2.1 CVV/CVC calculation and CVKs* for the service code of 000 and is printed on the card. The cardholder enters this value during the payment to confirm access to the card itself.

Both methods share the deficiency of becoming unreliable if leaked. If the address and the CVV_2 value of the card become known to a fraudster via an improperly secured website, they can be used to perform online transactions many times.

4.3.2 Overview

At a certain point, a private company has developed a new method for cardholder authentication in the online environment. The method, later renamed "3D Secure," delegated the cardholder authentication to the issuer [47].

The high-level flow of a 3D Secure authentication was as follows:

1. A *merchant plug-in(MPI)* is invoked during the payment process before submitting the transaction for authorization on an eCommerce website.

2. The merchant plug-in facilitates a request to a scheme directory service to locate the issuer's *access control server (ACS)*.

3. The directory service looks up the issuer ACS URL. If none is available or the issuer is unavailable, the directory service may provide stand-in authentication for the request (also called the "attempts" service).

4. The user on the eCommerce website is redirected to the ACS URL. Alternatively, the issuer web page is displayed embedded into the website.

5. The user interacts with the issuer's ACS to confirm identity. Initially, the users were required to remember and enter a password, but later the systems shited to one-time passwords communicated via a text message to the phone number on file. The authentication method itself was not in the scope of the 3D Secure standard, and each issuer could choose their preferred methods to authenticate the cardholder.

6. Upon completion of the interaction, the ACS would generate a cryptographical evidence value, called *authentication value, cardholder authentication verification value (CAVV)*, or *universal cardholder authentication field (UCAF)*, for the authentication and redirect the user back to the eCommerce website to proceed with the payment.

7. The eCommerce website would then communicate the CAVV to the payment gateway together with the transaction authorization request.

This method drove the fraud down and thus provided a formidable extra layer of security for online payments. It was adopted under the "Verified By Visa" brand name by Visa and then licensed out to other card schemes.

It did have several drawbacks. For one, the customers did not like to make the extra authentication step, and the deployment of 3D Secure led to card abandonment. Furthermore, the eCommerce website had no way of knowing the authentication status once the user was forwarded to the ACS. If the authentication was completed successfully or failed, the user returned, but otherwise, abandonment of the checkout flow was indistinguishable from a technical fault in the process. Finally, with the ascendance of smartphones, the older forms of redirection and inline frames became inadequate for a modern mobile shopping experience.

To combat the user fallout, issuers started implementing a *frictionless flow*, where the cardholder was redirected to the issuer ACS, then the ACS would make a risk-based decision and possibly redirect the cardholder back without any interactive authentication steps. It brought significant value and allowed 3D Secure to become ubiquitous in places like the United Kingdom.

The card payment industry, via the EMV standards body, had considered the drawbacks and the new developments and defined a new, open standard called EMV 3-D Secure [66].

For example, the standard includes an additional message from the ACS back to the intermediate directory service with the authentication result, which now addresses cases when the cardholder abandoned the authentication.

The frictionless flow and its opposite, the *challenge flow*, were made an integral part of the standard, removing the need to actually redirect the user if the issuer agrees to authenticate without any user interaction.

In order to simplify the issuer's decision on frictionless authentication, the standard has added an optional step of device fingerprinting. The consumer would be silently redirected to the issuer ACS, which would capture the source IP and additional browser characteristics. If found matching the previously authenticated transactions, this additional information can lead the issuer to agree to a frictionless flow. In addition, an out-of-band (decoupled) authentication is supported: for example, the issuer can opt to confirm the payment by sending a push notification to the issuer app on the cardholder's phone.

The standard also introduces support for mobile applications, allowing support for a native interface rendered by the app instead of the issuer ACS.

4.3.3 Key entities and protocol security

There are three participants in a 3-D Secure interaction, each belonging to its domain (hence the name, Three Domains). There is the *acquirer domain*, the scheme (also known as the *interoperability domain*), and the *issuer domain*.

The acquirer domain contains the *3DS Server*. It handles online requests. The 3DS server communicates with the scheme domain's *Directory Server (DS)*. The Directory Server contains a directory of issuer ACS addresses and re-routes 3DS Server requests to the correct ACS. Finally, the *Access Control Server (ACS)* lies in the issuer domain.

A full 3-D Secure interaction flow is as follows: the requestor app on the mobile phone, or the eCommerce website, connects to the 3DS Server to initiate the flow. The 3DS server knows the address where the ACS would like to collect browser fingerprints and can redirect the requesting browser to that address before proceeding with the authentication flow.

The 3DS Server sends an *authentication request* (AReq) message to the Directory Server, which relays it to the appropriate ACS. If a challenge is required (i.e., if the ACS would like to interact with the cardholder directly for authentication), the client (requestor app or the website) is notified via the *authentication response* (ARes) message and is redirected to the ACS for the challenge interaction. The challenge interaction uses *challenge request* (CReq) and *challenge response* (CRes) messages. Upon completing the challenge interaction, the ACS

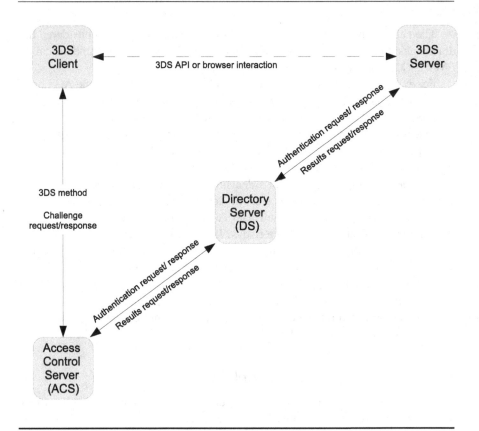

Figure 4.2: 3D Secure overview.

sends a *results request* (RReq) to the Directory Server, which forwards it to the 3DS Server. See Figure 4.2.

4.3.4 TLS requirements

There are, therefore, two types of links in the protocol. The first type is internal links between the 3DS entities such as the 3DS Server, DS, and the ACS. The other type is the external links between the requestor app or the browser to the ACS.

For internal links, the 3DS standard mandates TLS usage and defines the following requirements:

1. The TLS connection must be mutually authenticated (see *Section 4.1.3 Server parameters*).

2. The list of specific cipher suites, including the elliptic curve which must be used, is provided as part of the standard [66].

3. The certificate format is X.509.

4. The Directory Server must define a CA and sign all certificates. Only certificates signed by the particular DS are allowed in communication between entities of the card scheme to which the DS belongs.

For external links, since a generic browser will be connecting to the ACS, the latter should use a commercial certificate and a commercial CA generally known to browsers, also enforcing TLS.

4.3.5   Application-level security

The standard provides support for mobile app authentication and imposes additional requirements for the security of the message exchange between the mobile app and the ACS. Since the standard specifies an SDK for mobile applications, it speaks of interaction between the SDK and the ACS rather than between the app and the ACS.

There are two key points in an app's interaction (called in the standard *app-based flow*) with the rest of the 3-D Secure environment, requiring additional application-level security on top of the transport-level encryption provided by the TLS protocol.

The device app collects device information before submitting the initial request to begin the authentication. The app must know which Directory Server will handle the authentication request and possess the public key of that Directory Server.

The public key can be an RSA key or an elliptic curve key. In the first case, the app encrypts the device data using the DS public key in the OAEP mode (see *Section 1.8.1 Padding and cipher block chaining*). In the second case, the app generates an ephemeral key pair, conducts a Diffie-Hellman key exchange, encrypts the content using the generated key, and deletes the ephemeral key.

The format for encrypted messages and the key exchange is according to the JSON Web Encryption (JWE) standard (see *Section 4.2.4 JSON web encryption (JWE)*). In this case, the Key Encryption mode is used.

The result is included in the first message to the 3DS Server, which forwards it to the Directory Server, which, in its turn, decrypts the data and sends it to the ACS in an unencrypted form.

In addition to the device information, the app prepares a set of keys that will be used in its communication with the ACS in case a challenge is required. According to the standard, the app will have to establish a secure channel with the ACS. It is done by performing a two-way elliptic curve Diffie Hellman key exchange and using the JWE CEK in the Direct Key Agreement mode.

The app prepares a key pair (Q_C, d_C) and shares Q_C as a JWK in the initial message (see *Section 4.2.2 JSON web key (JWK)*).

The ACS generates its own key pair (Q_T, d_T) on the ACS side. The server possesses a key pair and a certificate for it, signed by the Directory Server CA. If the server requires a challenge, it performs the following steps:

1. Signs the received ephemeral key Q_C, its own ephemeral key Q_T, and the URL for the secure channel with its private key.

2. Generates two encryption keys based on the elliptic curve Diffie Hellman exchange process, one for each direction. See *Section 1.6.2 Elliptic curve Diffie-Hellman (ECDH)* for the secret establishment process description.

3. Includes the signature and the certificate in the response message.

The key generation process for the encryption of the initial device information and the subsequent challenge flow is using the Concat KDF method (see *Section 1.10.2 ConcatKDF key derivation function*) with the following parameters:

■ Key data length is 256.

■ AlgorithmID is an empty string (meaning that only four 0x00 bytes of length are transmitted as an empty value indicator).

■ PartyUIInfo is an empty string. Likewise, four zero bytes indicate the absence of value.

■ PartyVInfo is an ASCII string with either the directory server ID or the reference number of the app SDK, depending on the specific use case. Both values are also transmitted in the clear alongside the key.

■ SuppPubInfo is the 32-bit key data length value, 0x0000 0100.

■ SuppPrivInfo is empty.

The outgoing CReq is encrypted and signed using either AES 128 in the GCM mode (see *Section 1.9.6 Galois/Counter mode*) or AES 128 in CBC mode with SHA-256 HMAC signature and is sent according to the JWE representation (see *Section 4.2.4 JSON web encryption (JWE)*). The response CRes is encrypted and signed using one of the same methods but with a different key.

Chapter 5

Protecting the PIN

5.1 Introduction

The card schemes use the PIN entry as the ultimate method to authenticate the cardholder. It does, indeed, introduce a second-factor authentication to an in-store card payment: if the card itself is a *possession factor* ("something you have"), the PIN is a *knowledge factor* ("something you know").

Because of that, the PIN value is considered the most sensitive part of a card payment transaction. Special physical and logical requirements apply to devices that capture the PIN entered by the cardholder.

The legacy method of PIN verification values (see *Section 3.2.2 PVV, PVKs, and PVKI*) would not allow the change of the PIN by the cardholder. Furthermore, it is limited to four digits PINs and is not collision-free.

The chip on the card can validate the PIN without turning to the issuer (see *Sections 3.4.3.1 PIN block format 2 and offline plaintext validation* and *3.4.3.2 Encrypted offline PIN*). However, relying solely on the offline PIN validation is risky: for example, without communicating with the issuer, the card may not know that the issuer has blocked it.

Since multiple hosts relay the transaction on its path to the issuer, steps should be taken to ensure that none of the intermediaries can learn the PIN. Furthermore, POS devices operate in a generally unsafe environment of the merchant store, so their level of trust is limited. It is a classical problem for cryptography to solve.

DOI: 10.1201/9781003371366-5

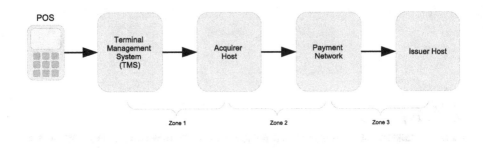

Figure 5.1: Zone management for PIN translation.

The industry relies primarily on symmetric cryptography to protect the PIN values in transit. Besides having much shorter keys, symmetric algorithms are much faster for similar cryptographic strength. The PCI PIN standard allows TDES with double or triple keys and AES for PIN block encryption. However, it is impossible to establish mutual secrets between every possible terminal and issuer with thousands of financial institutions and multitudes of POS devices.

5.2 Zoning

In order to address the challenges, the payment network is segmented into logical zones. Each zone begins or terminates at an acquirer or an issuer host. The host is responsible for maintaining security within its zone. Each zone uses its own key or keys for encrypted PIN blocks. Before sending the EPB to another entity (scheme or host), the sender ensures that the EPB is encrypted with the appropriate key defined for the next zone (see Figure 5.1).

The key used to encrypt PIN blocks within a particular zone is called the *zone PIN key* (*ZPK*) or *worker key* (*WK*, with *AWK* used for the *acquirer worker key* and *IWK* for the *issuer worker key*), or a *PIN encryption key* (*PEK*). Within one zone, the host would operate on a key under a ZPK. Before sending the key to a second zone, the host must decrypt the key with the first ZPK and encrypt it with the second ZPK. This process is called PIN translation.

In order to make it impossible for the host to learn the PIN block in the middle of PIN translation, the PCI PIN standard prescribes performing this operation using a dedicated secure device, the *hardware security module* (*HSM*).

However, for the HSM to be able to translate PIN encryption, it must somehow learn the two ZPKs to use. These, too, can be compromised in transit. Therefore, the ZPKs themselves are transmitted while being encrypted by another key. That other key is called the *zone master key* (*ZMK*), *transport key*, or *key encryption key* (*KEK*).

While the HSM devices can perform secure operations fast, resist tampering, and lock upon detection of suspicious activity, they are not designed to store a large number of keys. An HSM would store a limited number of *local master keys (LMK)* or *master file keys (MFK)*.

Any key that the HSM operates upon or works with can only exist outside of the HSM if encrypted by the HSM's local key or the zone master key.

5.2.1 PIN translation

A processing host would store worker keys in a regular database encrypted with the HSM local key (LMK). Upon each invocation of an HSM operation, the host would load the encrypted key from its database and pass it to the HSM as part of its input.

For example, if the acquirer zone uses ZPK_1 and the payment network uses ZPK_2, the acquiring host stores ZPK_1 and ZPK_2 encrypted with the LMK. Whenever it needs to translate the EPB from encryption with ZPK_1 to encryption with ZPK_2, the acquiring host sends to the HSM the EPB itself and the two encrypted ZPKs (see Figure 5.2). The HSM would then:

1. Decrypt ZPK_1.

2. Decrypt ZPK_2.

3. Decrypt the EPB with ZPK_1 and check its format.

4. Encrypt the EPB with ZPK_2.

5. Return the new EPB to the acquiring host.

The new EPB will then be ready for transmission to the payment network since it is encrypted with the correct ZPK, the ZPK_2. Note that at no point in this flow does the host have access to a clear-text ZPK or a clear-text PIN.

5.2.2 Key exchange and management

Prior to any PIN translation, the ZPKs must somehow become encrypted with the LMK and then find their way to the host database while at all times being encrypted by a key. These operations are called *key import* and *key export*.

During the key export operation, the HSM receives a key under its LMK, decrypts it, then encrypts it with a transport key, and outputs the result.

During the key import operation, the HSM receives a key under some transport key (ZMK), decrypts it, encrypts it with its local key, and outputs the result

It helps to consider the ZPK as existing in two forms: for local use and interzonal transportation. The ZPK under LMK is for the host's use, and only the encrypting HSM or its clones can possibly use it. The ZPK under ZMK is for

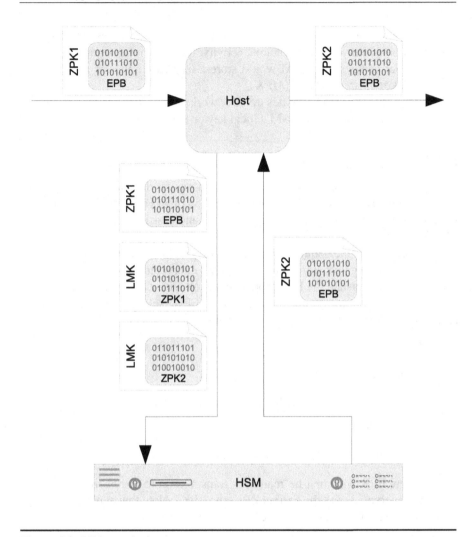

Figure 5.2: PIN translation.

inter-zonal transportation, and any HSM in another zone which has previously imported the ZMK can also use the ZPK.

Since outside an HSM, both the ZMK and the ZPK exist only in the encrypted form, the *key check value* (*KCV*) was defined to help users confirm key identity and validity. For TDES keys, the key check value can be generated by encrypting an input vector of zero bytes (0x00) and taking the first few digits of the result, at most 6, or by calculating a CMAC of a zero input block (see *Section 1.9.1 CMAC*) and taking the first 10 digits. For AES keys, only the CMAC method is used.

The HSM also can create a new ZPK and output it under the LMK and under a transport key so that the locally encrypted value can be entered into the host database while the value under the transport key can be sent to the owner of the next zone for deployment. This operation is called *key generation*.

However, to know the ZMK, the HSM also needs it encrypted under the LMK.

This challenge is addressed by allowing recombination of ZMKs from multiple clear-text components, usually by XORing the values. The operation is called *forming the key*. Since it is the most sensitive step of a key exchange process, the PCI PIN standard elaborates on the procedures surrounding it. For example, there must be at least three clear-text components borne by three separate key custodians and typed into the HSM while no surveillance is possible.

In the chronological order, the process of establishing a mutual ZPK between two zones, Zone 1 and Zone 2, may look as follows:

1. Key custodians in Zone 1 gather and generate three clear-text components of the ZMK, taking care not to expose or compromise these components.

2. Key custodians in Zone 1 form the ZMK from the components.

3. The HSM in Zone 1 encrypts the ZMK with its local master key, LMK_1, and outputs the result.

4. Key custodians in Zone 1 safely send the clear-text components to custodians in Zone 2, typically using paper sheets and tamper-evident envelopes.

5. Key custodians in Zone 2 gather and form the ZMK from the clear-text components by using the HSM, which XORs the values.

6. The HSM encrypts the ZMK with its local master key, LMK_2, and outputs the result.

At this point, each party possesses a copy of the ZMK, encrypted with the respective local key. The parties can now exchange the ZPKs freely since they can ship these keys encrypted by the shared ZMK.

In some solutions, an automated protocol can communicate the current ZPK from a host to its counterpart, rotating it periodically. The process is possible since the ZPK always arrives while encrypted with a manually established mutual ZMK. The process is also called *dynamic key exchange* (*DKE*).

In a less automated setting, one of the parties, let us assume Zone 1, follows the steps below:

1. The owner of Zone 1 invokes the HSM key generation function, providing the ZMK under LMK_1 as an input parameter.

2. The HSM generates a new ZPK and prints it in two representations: encrypted by its LMK, LMK_1, and by the ZMK.

3. The ZPK value under LMK$_1$ can be deployed in the host's database in Zone 1.

4. The ZPK, encrypted with the ZMK, can be sent to the owner of Zone 2.

5. The owner of Zone 2 receives the ZPK under the ZMK and invokes the HSM key import function, providing ZPK under the ZMK and ZMK under LMK$_2$ as the parameters.

6. The HSM in Zone 2 decrypts the ZMK using its local key, LMK$_2$.

7. The HSM in Zone 2 decrypts the ZPK with the ZMK it has recovered.

8. The HSM in Zone 2 encrypts the ZPK with its local key, LMK$_2$.

9. The output is provided to the owner of Zone 2, who then deploys ZPK under LMK$_2$ in the host database.

5.3 Key Encryption and Representation

The PCI PIN standard approves two algorithms for PIN encryption and the encryption of keys, the TDES and the AES. The key encryption algorithm must be at least as strong as the PIN encryption algorithm. For example, if the ZPK is an AES key, only AES must be used to encrypt the ZPK.

The standard method to represent and store PIN keys is storing its hexadecimal value, encoded in ASCII, with a single letter prefix, or tag, indicating the format. In other words, if the first byte of the key is 0xED, it will be stored as the two ASCII letters 'E' and 'D', i.e., as two bytes 0x4544.

5.3.1 X9.17 and variant formats

For DES keys, one widespread key encryption method for DES keys is the ANSI X9.17 [67]. The scheme typically uses the tag of X for double-length and Y for triple-length DES keys.

Under this method, the key is encrypted using TDES in the EDE/ECB mode, and the result is stored as-is, with an appropriate tag prepended to it.

While being interoperable and very simple to implement, the scheme is considered weak due to the considerations listed below.

An attacker can potentially intercept many encrypted PIN blocks and then use them to learn something about the ZPK used to encrypt them. To protect against this type of attack, ZPKs are rotated periodically (with an automated solution, they can be rotated very frequently).

Due to the established ZMK, which was not transmitted using any electronic channels, the ZPK rotation remains secure for a long time.

If a transport key is also used as a worker key, this exposes the transport key to this type of attack and jeopardizes key transmission and rotation security.

Therefore, the PCI PIN standard requires that the processes for key management separate keys by type, and there are measures to ensure that a key of a particular type cannot be used for another purpose.

With the X9.17 key encryption method, this requirement can only be met via method and procedure.

An alternative that came into widespread use was to implement *variants*. The variant is a predefined value that is XORed with the key encryption key prior to encryption of each part of the input.

For example, if the input (a ZPK) is double-length, then there will be two masks, XOR-ed with the KEK prior to encryption of the first and the second half of the ZPK. For an example of a variant calculation, see *Section D.2 Variant Key Encryption.*

The applied variant differs per key type and also per key part. In other words, the halves or thirds of the key cannot be used in a different order since, with a high degree of probability, the parity check on the decrypted key will fail.

Since AES keys have no parity bits, this method is only applicable to TDES keys.

The variant method is no longer recommended for use and is being phased out by the PCI PIN standard and card schemes in favor of the key block method.

For clarity, the key encrypted into a key block is referred to as the *payload.*

5.3.2   Key block

There are several key block formats in use. The ASC X9 defined the TR-31 format [68]. Some HSM vendors also support a proprietary format for key blocks alongside the standard one.

All key blocks consist of the *key block header* (*KBH*), the *encrypted key block* (*EKB*), and the MAC that binds the KBH and the EKB. The key used for encryption and calculation of the MAC is called the *key block protection key.*

The key block is an application of the AEAD approach (see *Section 1.9.5 Authenticated encryption*) to the encryption of cryptographic keys: the data is encrypted and signed, while the header is sent in the clear.

5.3.2.1   Key block header

Vendor-specific documentation should be consulted for the details of each proprietary key block format. The standard TR 31 blocks are secure and supported by all major HSM brands and, therefore, recommended for use over proprietary formats.

The block header contains the following details:

■   Key block version ID and key block length.

■ Key usage. Specifies the intended usage of the payload. 'P0' indicates PIN encryption (corresponds to ZPK), and 'K1' indicates that the key is used as a TR-31 key block protection key, corresponding to ZMK.

■ Algorithm. Specifies the algorithm used to encrypt the payload. The value of 'T' corresponds to the TDES, 'A' for AES, with other algorithms and proprietary values supported, too.

■ Mode of use. Specifies how the payload may be used. For example, PIN encryption key (ZPK) and key block protection key (in our case, ZMK) may support the modes 'B' – both encrypt and decrypt, 'D' – decrypt only, and 'E' – encrypt only.

■ Key version number. Specifies the payload version number. This field has two alphanumeric characters. If the field begins with the lowercase letter 'c', the key block does not carry a key but rather a component of a key.

■ Exportability. The payload export (in a sense mentioned in *Section 5.2.2 Key exchange and management*) can be prohibited by setting 'N' in this header field. Alternatively, the key export can be allowed under a KEK.

■ Optional blocks information and the optional blocks themselves. These values are specific per implementation but are also protected by the MAC.

5.3.2.2 Encryption and authentication (Binding)

The key block protection key is not actually used to encrypt the payload data and generate the MAC. Instead, it serves as a basis for generating two other keys.

These two keys are called the *key block encryption key* and the *key block MAC key*.

The standard describes two methods to generate these keys: a *derivation* method suitable for TDES and AES and a *variant* method suitable only for TDES.

Depending on the key derivation method, the block encryption and signing – the process which the standard calls "binding" – differ.

The payload binding with keys obtained using the key derivation method follows (see also Figure 5.3).

1. The payload to be encrypted (in our case, the ZPK) is padded with random bytes to a multiple of 8 bytes. The payload can be padded with more than 8 bytes to obscure the actual length of the key.

2. Two bytes of key length, the actual payload key, and the padding are concatenated into the input vector V.

3. CMAC value, M, is calculated for $H \parallel V$ using the key block MAC key.

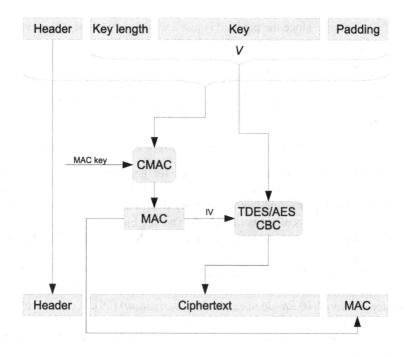

Figure 5.3: Key block binding.

4. The key length, the payload, and the padding (value of V without the header) are encrypted with CBC TDES encryption. The key block encryption key is used as the encryption key. The value M is the initialization vector for the CBC encryption: $C = E_{K,M}(V)$.

5. The key block is formed by the concatenation of the header, the output of the encryption, and the MAC: $KB = H \parallel C \parallel M$.

The key block is generated as follows for keys derived using the variant key method:

1. The payload to be encrypted (in our case, the ZPK) is padded with random bytes to a multiple of 8 bytes. The payload can be padded with more than 8 bytes to obscure the actual length of the key.

2. Two bytes of key length, the actual payload key, and the padding are concatenated into the input vector V.

3. V is encrypted with CBC TDES with the key block encryption key. If there are not at least 42 random bits in the first block of the payload, a random IV is generated and added to the key block header. In the case of

the payments, since the payload is just a worker key, all of it is considered random.

4. CBC-MAC value, M, is calculated on $H \parallel V$.

5. The key block is formed by concatenating the header, the output of the encryption, and the MAC: $KB = H \parallel C \parallel M$.

5.3.2.3 *Key block encryption key and key block MAC key generation*

The standard specifies two possible methods for generating keys: variant and derivation. With the variant method, the key block encryption key is obtained from the key block protection key by XORing it with the value of 'EEEEEEEE' (8 bytes of 0x45) across all parts of the key. The key block MAC key is obtained by XORing the key block protection key with the value of 'MMMMMMMM' (8 bytes of 0x4D).

The derivation method for generating keys uses similar principles for TDES and AES protocols, in compliance with the NIST KDF method in the counter mode (see *Section 1.10 Randomness and key derivation*) [69]. A data vector with a running counter is fed as the input to the CMAC algorithm, with the key block protection key being the algorithm's key. The procedure repeats until enough bits for the target key length are generated.

The input data for both TDES and AES keys contains:

1. A counter for blocks of the output, starting at 1. For example, if a triple-length TDES key is being derived using the TDES algorithm, the counter traverses values of 0x01, 0x02, and 0x03 for every 8 bytes being output. Since AES keys are 128, 192, or 256 bit, the counter for the AES derivation tracks 16-byte outputs and can only assume values of 0x01 and 0x02.

2. The label – in this case, an indicator of the key usage, with 0x0000 indicating that the encryption key is being generated and the value of 0x0001 corresponding to the MAC key.

3. A separator byte of 0x00.

4. The context value – an indicator of the algorithm which will use the derived key, with 0x0000 and 0x0001 corresponding to double and triple-length TDES keys and values of 0x0002 through 0x0004 corresponding to AES keys.

5. Length, in bits, of the keying material generated for the derived key. E.g., 0x0080 for double-length TDES or 128-bit AES keys.

Each round of the algorithm outputs 64 (for DES) or 128 (for AES) bits. The desired number of bits is then taken from the output. I.e., for the AES algorithm, the full output of the first round and the first 8 bytes of the second round will be used.

Since the TDES algorithm ignores parity bits in the key, they may or may not be corrected after the derivation round, depending on whether the implementation of the algorithm will reject a key with incorrect parity bits.

An example derivation of the keys can be found in *D.3 Key Block Key Derivation*.

5.4 Derived Unique Key Per Transaction (DUKPT)

5.4.1 Design considerations

The Derived Unique Key Per Transaction (DUKPT) algorithm secures the exchange of messages between terminal endpoints and the next hop, usually the terminal management system [70] . The algorithm allows the derivation of keys for encryption of PIN blocks as well as keys for encryption and authentication of data.

Two flavors of the algorithm exist, the TDES and the AES DUKPT, with TDES being the earlier of the two, designated to be supplanted by the AES DUKPT in the future.

Payment hosts reside in a tightly controlled environment and can deploy and securely operate HSMs to safeguard encryption keys while communicating over secure network channels. On the contrary, POS devices, which are many and are deployed on merchant's premises, are inherently less secure. Furthermore, the communications between the POS and the host are much easier to intercept.

If a single key is shared across devices or the same key is repeatedly used to encrypt PIN blocks, an attacker can either gain access to the encryption key or eavesdrop on enough ciphertext to mount a successful attack.

A terminal cannot store unique keys for all future transactions and therefore requires a mechanism to generate them. Furthermore, the solution in which the acquiring host must store a unique derivation value per terminal is also best avoided.

An obvious next step is to create a *derivation hierarchy* (see Figure 5.4). The acquiring host creates and securely stores a *base derivation key* (*BDK*), from which all other keys are derived. Each terminal, in turn, receives a dedicated *initial key* (*IK*), from which all subsequent keys are derived. The initial key is sometimes, somewhat imprecisely, called the *initial PIN encryption key* or *IPEK*.

Finally, each terminal derives the encryption and authentication keys it needs from the initial key.

With this solution, the BDK is protected on the acquiring host side by security means such as the HSM. On the terminal side, a compromise of a single terminal will not lead to a compromise of the entire terminal network. However,

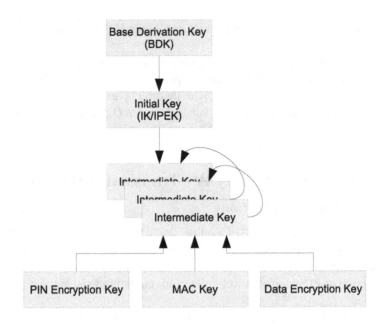

Figure 5.4: Derivation hierarchy.

an attacker can learn the IK and thus gain access to all future transactions from that terminal.

The key load process into terminals is called *key injection*, and the PCI PIN security standard(see *Section 6.2.1 PCI PIN standard*) contains strict requirements on the process itself and the facilities where it can take place. The goal is to protect the initial key.

There is a challenge with a sequential key derivation. While the terminal can store the last key and derive the next one from it in one derivation round, the acquiring host only stores the BDK. Therefore, it will first have to derive the IK and then repeat the key derivation steps as many times as that particular terminal processed transactions. Such a solution is not feasible.

Instead, the DUKPT protocol uses an ingenious method of key derivation, organizing the future keys into a tree. The acquiring host is guaranteed to reach any future key value with a limited number of iterations (10 for TDES and 16 for AES-based DUKPT), while the terminal itself stores several future keys in parallel, at any given time, using one of them to obtain the next encryption key.

Upon the key injection, the terminal generates its initial set of *future keys* (21 for TDES and 32 for AES-based DUKPT). At this point in time, the IK is no longer needed, and it can be deleted from the terminal, thus allowing for another layer of protection.

It is worth pointing out that the keys originating from the IK are not used as-is for data encryption and authentication. Instead, specific working keys are derived for each purpose. Therefore, these keys are called *intermediate derivation keys*.

A working key of TDES DUKPT is always a double-length TDES key. A working key of AES DUKPT can be either a double- or triple-length TDES key, an AES key, or an HMAC key.

The BDK is a double-length TDES key in the case of TDES DUKPT. In the case of AES DUKPT, the BDK is an AES key. Any TDES working key can be derived from an AES BDK, but only AES or HMAC keys of equal or lower strength are allowed. For example, a 128-bit AES BDK can be used to derive a triple-length TDES working key or a 128-bit AES working key, but not a 192 or a 256-bit AES working key.

To summarize, as part of the DUKPT algorithm, the keys are derived as follows:

■ The acquiring host generates the BDK key.

■ The initial keys (IKs) are derived by the acquiring host from the BDK and are loaded into each POS device.

■ The intermediate derivation key is generated per each transaction in the POS and the acquiring host.

  ■ The acquiring host derives the intermediate derivation key from the BDK.

  ■ The POS derives the intermediate derivation key from one of the future keys. The POS then discards one of the future keys and instead stores the intermediate derivation key.

■ The working keys used for PIN encryption, data encryption, and message authentication are derived from the intermediate derivation key.

The TDES DUKPT algorithm allows a certain number of transactions (see *Section 5.4.2 Key serial number (KSN)*) to be performed out of the same initial key. Once the number has been exhausted, the POS must be brought to a key injection facility to load a new initial key. The AES DUKPT algorithm allows deploying a new key when the old one has been exhausted. However, the supported number of transactions is quite high for a physical in-store terminal in both cases.

5.4.2 Key serial number (KSN)

Each key is assigned a unique *key serial number* called the *KSN*. Its size has changed between the TDES and the AES revisions of the algorithm, but the AES standard supports a KSN compatibility mode.

In the TDES version, the KSN has a total length of 10 bytes (80 bits) and the following structure:

■ Key Set ID (*KSI*) – an identifier of the particular BDK used for this key, 5 bytes.

■ PED ID – an identifier of the specific PED device. Its length is 19 bits (4 bytes and 3 bits).

■ Transaction counter – a running counter of the keys derived within each device, 21 bits.

The concatenation of the KSI and the PED ID in the TDES version constitutes the initial key ID and is called "legacy initial key ID" in the standard documentation.

In the AES mode, the KSN has a total length of 12 bytes (96 bits), and its structure is as follows:

■ BDK ID – an identifier of the particular BDK used for this key, 4 bytes.

■ Derivation ID – an identifier of the specific initial key as derived from this BDK. Note that instead of explicitly defining this part of the initial key ID as the device identifier, the new standard uses a broader term of "derivation."

■ Transaction counter – 4 bytes (32 bits) are the transaction counter.

In the KSN compatibility mode, the KSI and the PED ID are padded with 4 bits from the left and 1 bit from the right to the length of 64 bits and placed in the initial key ID part of the AES KSN. The transaction counter is left-padded with 11 bits and is placed in the transaction counter part of the AES KSN. See also Figure 5.5.

The KSN must be sent alongside each transaction from the PED device for the acquiring host to reconstruct the keys used with the transaction.

The transaction counter for the TDES algorithm has 21 bits. However, only values with a bit cardinality of 10 or less are allowed, and the POS will skip values with more set bits than that. The total maximum number of transactions for TDES DUKPT is slightly over 1 million transactions.[1]

The AES algorithm supports the same number of transactions in the KSN compatibility mode. However, the native KSN value of the AES DUKPT has 32 bits, allows maximum cardinality of 16, and supports over 2.4 billion transactions from a single initial key.[2] Furthermore, the AES DUKPT algorithm allows sending of a new initial key to the terminal without the need to take the terminal back to an injection facility.

---

[1] The exact number is $\sum_{i=0}^{k} \binom{n}{i} = \sum_{i=0}^{10} \binom{21}{i} = 1,048,576$

[2] The exact number is $\sum_{i=0}^{k} \binom{n}{i} = \sum_{i=0}^{16} \binom{32}{i} = 2,448,023,843$

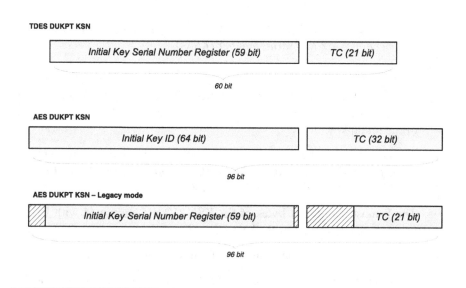

Figure 5.5: KSN structure.

A device that implements the TDES DUKPT algorithm may not send the full KSN with every transaction. In that case, the KSN will be left-padded with 0xFF by the acquiring host. Since this operation affects the derivation of the initial key (see *Section 5.4.3 Initial key derivation*), for such devices, the padded KSN should also be used for the generation of the IK before key injection.

5.4.3   Initial key derivation

In both algorithms, the derivation of the initial key differs from the subsequent intermediate derivation keys. However, the extent of the difference varies: with TDES, the implementation of the IK derivation cannot be reused to generate the subsequent keys since the method differs.

With AES, the key derivation follows the standard process (see *Section 1.10 Randomness and Key Derivation*), and the difference between the initial and the subsequent keys is in a few bytes of the initial input value.

However, there is a certain commonality between the methods: in both cases, the initial key uses the most significant bytes of the KSN (where the key set/BDK and the device identification are) while the subsequent keys use the least significant bytes (where the transaction counter is stored).

The following description of the initial key derivation applies to the generation of the IK prior to key injection and its generation while handling a transaction from the device.

The TDES initial key derivation works as follows (the BDK is a double-length TDES key):

1. The KSN is left-padded with 0xFF to the full length of 10 bytes if needed (see *Section 5.4.2 Key serial number (KSN)*).

2. The 21 least significant bytes of the KSN are set to zero.

3. The 8 most significant bytes of the KSN (V) are encrypted with TDES using the BDK as the key: $IK_1 = E_{BDK}(V)$. The result, IK_1, is the left half of the initial key.

4. A variant is applied to the BDK: both of its halves are XORed with the fixed value of 0xC0C0C0C0 00000000: $BDK' = BDK \oplus$ 0xC0C0C0C000000000C0C0C0C000000000.

5. The 8 most significant bytes of the KSN (V) are encrypted with TDES using the BDK variant as the key: $IK_2 = E_{BDK'}(V)$.

6. The initial key is the concatenation of the two values: $IK = IK_1 \parallel IK_2$.

7. Since the parity bits do not affect the TDES computation, the IK may or may not be adjusted for parity.

The AES initial key derivation algorithm uses the counter mode of the standard key derivation function, as defined in NIST 800-108 [27] (see *Section 1.10 Randomness and Key Derivation*). However, since the input length is identical to the AES block size, the PRF is an AES encryption, not a CMAC computation. Furthermore, the input value to the PRF is slightly different.

The BDK is an AES key of a standard size. The AES encryption algorithm receives the BDK as its key and the derivation data as the input block. The first 8-byte block of the derivation data for the initial key is as follows:

■ Constant byte, 0x01.

■ Key block counter, 0x01 for the first and 0x02 for the second iteration of the algorithm if applicable.

■ Key usage indicator, 0x8001 (Key Derivation, Initial key).

■ Algorithm indicator of the algorithm that is going to use the derived key: 0x0002 for AES-128, 0x0003 for AES-192, and 0x0004 for AES-256.

■ Length of the derived key in bits, 0x0080, 0x00C0, and 0x0100 for AES-128, 192, and 256, correspondingly.

The second 8-byte block of the derivation data is the 8 leftmost bytes of the initial KSN. Note that, considering the KSN structure, these bytes will contain the BDK ID and the Derivation ID in the full AES mode and the KSI and the PED ID in the KSN compatibility mode (see also *Section 5.7*).

The input value is generated as above and provided as the input to the AES encryption, alongside the BDK as the key, up to two times. For 192-bit keys, the last 4 bytes of the second output are discarded.

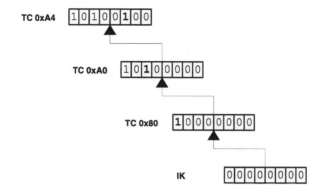

Figure 5.6: Intermediate key derivation.

5.4.4 Intermediate key derivation

The most exciting part of the DUKPT algorithm is the intermediate key derivation. While the bit sizes and the actual derivation functions differ between the
TDES and the AES version of the DUKPT algorithm, the same robust principle
remains identical.

Since the sequential derivation of the next key from the previous one is not
feasible on the acquiring host side, a derivation tree is used instead.

The rule for key derivation is as follows: a key corresponding to a particular transaction counter is derived from a key that corresponds to a value of the
counter with its rightmost bit unset. (see Figure 5.6)

For example, let us assume that the transaction counter has the binary value
of 10100100, having the decimal value of 164 (0xA4). The rightmost set bit here
is the third one, corresponding to the value of 0x4 in the rightmost nibble of
the value. The key for this transaction counter will be derived from the value of
1010000 (160 or 0xA0), with that rightmost bit unset.

The key for the transaction counter of 10100000 (160 or 0xA0) was previously derived from the key for transaction 10000000 (128, or 0x80). Finally, the
key for 1000000 was derived from the IK.

The derivation process of the intermediate key differs from that of the initial
key. Furthermore, in the TDES DUKPT, this process differs from the standard
TDES encryption.

5.4.4.1 TDES DUKPT intermediate key derivation

The TDES intermediate key is derived from a previous key, K. As these are
double-length keys, assume $K = K_1 \parallel K_2$, where K_1 is the left and K_2 is the right
half of the key.

The derivation process operates on a register R of 16 bytes, consisting of two halves, R_1 and R_2.

The process proceeds as follows:

1. The key from which the new key is derived is loaded into K.

2. The rightmost 64 bits of the KSN value for which the key is to be derived are loaded into R_1.

3. The right half of the key, K_2, is XORed with R_1 and is loaded into R_2: $R_2 = R_1 \oplus K_2$.

4. The right half of the register, R_2, is encrypted with DES, using the left half of K, K_1, as the key: $R_2 = Enc_{K_1}(R_2)$.

5. The key register is XORed with a mask, C0C0C0C0000000: $K = K \oplus$ C0C0C0C0000000C0C0C0C0000000.

6. The left half of the register, R_1, is encrypted with DES, using the right half of K, K_2, as the key: $R_1 = Enc_{K_2}(R_1)$.

7. The left half of the register, R_1, is XORed with the right half of K, K_2: $R_1 = R_1 \oplus K_2$.

8. The result, $R = R_1 \parallel R_2$, is the freshly derived intermediate key.

5.4.4.2 AES DUKPT intermediate key derivation

The AES DUKPT intermediate key derivation differs slightly from the AES initial key derivation. The actual computation is identical, but the input value differs in two parts: the key usage indicator is 0x8000 (Key Derivation) and not 0x8001, and the rightmost 8 bytes of the value are composed of the rightmost 8 bytes of the KSN, rather than the leftmost.

The first 8-byte block of the derivation data for the intermediate key is as follows:

■ Constant byte, 0x01.

■ Key block counter, 0x01 for the first and 0x02 for the second iteration of the algorithm if applicable.

■ Key usage indicator, 0x8000 (Key Derivation).

■ Algorithm indicator of the algorithm that is going to use the derived key: 0x0002 for AES-128, 0x0003 for AES-192, and 0x0004 for AES-256.

■ Length of the derived key in bits, 0x0080, 0x00C0, and 0x0100 for AES-128, 192, and 256, correspondingly.

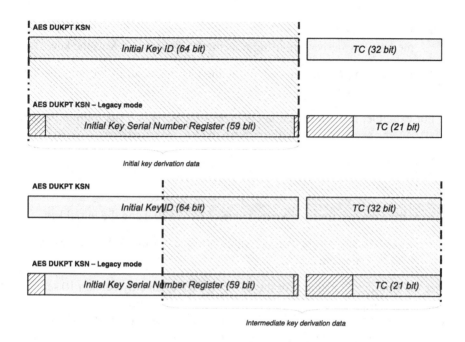

Figure 5.7: KSN for initial and intermediate key derivation.

The second 8-byte block of the derivation data is the 8 rightmost bytes of the initial KSN. Considering the KSN structure (see figure 5.7), these bytes will contain the Derivation ID and the transaction counter in the full AES mode, and the transaction counter and the rightmost 31 bits of the legacy initial key ID in the KSN compatibility mode.

5.4.4.3 Acquiring host intermediate key derivation

On the acquiring host side, the algorithm for the intermediate key derivation would therefore look as follows:

■ Upon obtaining the transaction, use the provided metadata and the KSN to identify and retrieve the correct BDK.

■ Derive the initial key, following the procedure described in *Section 5.4.3 Initial key derivation*, and load it into the register K.

■ Prepare the register R, loading the received KSN value into it and resetting the transaction counter of the KSN (the rightmost 21 bits) to zero.

■ Starting with the rightmost bit of the input KSN, scan the KSN value for set bits.

■ If a bit is set in the input KSN, set it in the register R. Perform the intermediate key derivation, using R as the KSN input and K as the key.

■ Replace the K with the value obtained as the result of the intermediate key derivation.

For example, if the transaction counter of the KSN is 5 (its trailing bits are ...0101), the acquiring host will perform the following actions:

1. Load the BDK.

2. Derive the initial key, IK.

3. Derive the key for the counter value of ...0100 using the initial key.

4. Derive the key for the counter value of ...0101 using the previously derived intermediate key.

Since the transaction counter for the TDES DUKPT can only contain 10 set bits, this operation is guaranteed to only require at most 10 intermediate key derivation steps for the TDES version of the algorithm or the AES version algorithm in the KSN compatibility mode. The AES DUKPT is guaranteed to take no more than 16 intermediate key derivation steps.

5.4.4.4 Terminal intermediate key derivation

The real beauty of the DUKPT key derivation happens on the terminal side.

Once the initial key has been loaded into the terminal, it generates the future keys (21 for TDES and 32 for AES version) and disposes of the IK. For each subsequent transaction, one key is derived, and one of the previously generated keys is deleted, keeping the overall number of keys stored in the terminal constant.

Nevertheless, the terminal can arrive at precisely the same set of intermediate keys without the initial key and the derivation process that the acquiring host can perform.

The process is as follows. Upon obtaining the IK, the terminal derives 21 or 32 future keys, corresponding to all possible values of bit cardinality 1, i.e., 1...0000, 0...1000, 0...0100, 0...0010, ..., 0...0001, with only one bit set but in every possible position. Each future key is stored in a register whose number corresponds to this bit position, in the order listed above, from 21 to 1.

Imagine that they are situated left to right, from register 21 to register 1.

The derivation process continues as follows: upon request for a new intermediate key, the terminal checks the rightmost set bit of the KSN value. The terminal then uses the future key stored in that register to derive the working key.

Then, if the KSN has less than the maximum allowed number of bits set, the terminal derives future keys for all registers to the right of the future key it has just used and for KSN values obtained by setting the appropriate bit in

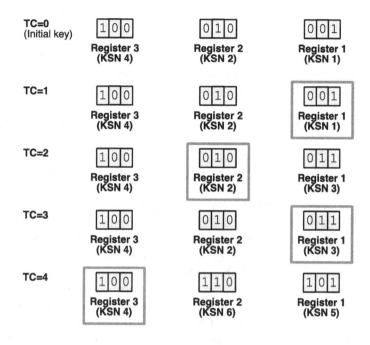

Figure 5.8: DUKPT terminal key derivation process – TCs 1 to 4.

the current KSN value. The terminal simply erases the key if the KSN has the maximum allowed number of bits set.

For example, if the terminal uses the KSN value of 12 (binary 1100), the rightmost bit of the KSN is bit 3. The terminal will then "iterate right" over bits 2 and 1 and generate keys for 14 (binary 1110) and 13 (1101), placing them in registers 2 and 1, accordingly.

To further illustrate, let us consider the case of three bits (see figure 5.8), and instead of derived keys, let us note just the KSN values to which these keys correspond. We will need three key registers and initially will generate future keys for values 4, 2, and 1, placing them in registers 3, 2, and 1.

For the first transaction, binary 001, there is a ready key in register 1. The terminal uses it and clears the register.

For the second transaction, binary 010, there is a ready key in register 2. The terminal uses it, then starts iterating to the right. In this case, the terminal turns on bit 1, obtains binary 011 or 3, generates the future key for this value, and stores it in register 1.

At this point, the terminal has just processed KSN 2 and has already prepared a future key for KSN 3. Its registers 3 and 1 have keys for KSN 4 and 3, correspondingly, and register 2 is empty.

KSN 3 is processed using the future key from register 1, and this key is discarded afterward.

KSN 4 (binary 100) is processed using the future key from register 3.

Upon using it, the terminal iterates rightwards, generating keys for 6 (110) and 5 (101) and placing them in registers 2 and 1. Then, the terminal deletes the key for KSN 4.

The value of KSN 5 is serviced by the already-prepared future key from register 1.

The value of KSN 6 (binary 110) is serviced from register 2. Then, the terminal iterates rightwards, generating the future key for KSN 7 (binary 111) in register 1 and deleting the key for KSN 6.

Finally, the value of KSN 7 is serviced from register 1 (see Figure 5.9).

While the description of the algorithm steps may be clear from the tabular form, it is still hard to understand why it succeeds. In order to understand the mechanics, let us represent the key derivation process as a directed graph of KSN values. It is acyclic and is, therefore, a tree.

Mapping the terminal key derivation process above to the tree helps see the following principles of the algorithm. We will use 4-bit values for that purpose.

If the KSN counter reached the KSN value of a particular initial future key, then all previous registers contain keys that were already used and can therefore be replaced. For example (see Figure 5.10), once the value of 4 (0100) has been reached, the previous values of 1, 2, and 3 have all been handled. Once the value of 8 has been reached, all values from 1 to 7 have been handled, and so on.

Iterating to the right replaces the values in these registers with the immediate children of the current KSN value in the tree. All other valid KSN values which are smaller than the current node value will be generated from these immediate children.

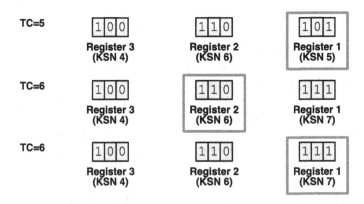

Figure 5.9: DUKPT terminal key derivation process – TCs 5 to 7.

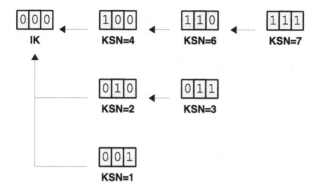

Figure 5.10: Derivation tree.

5.4.5 Working key derivation

The working key derivation uses the intermediate key, derived as shown above, to generate keys for PIN block encryption, message signature, and possible message encryption.

The DUKPT keys can be used to encrypt the PIN, encrypt the entire payment message, and compute a MAC for the entire payment message. Furthermore, the DUKPT keys can be used to authenticate and decrypt the messages coming from the acquiring host to the terminal (for example, as part of a point-to-point encryption implementation; see *Section 6.3 PCI Point-to-Point Encryption (P2PE)*).

Consequently, the algorithm allows the generation of working keys for PIN encryption, message authentication (request only and both ways), and data encryption (request only or both ways).

The TDES DUKPT working key derivation follows the variant paradigm for PIN encryption and message authentication keys. The key is generated by XOR-ing the intermediate key with a variant (flipping the last byte of each key half).

The TDES DUKPT key for data encryption is generated differently: using a two-step process. Assume $K = K_1 \parallel K_2$ is the derived intermediate key, and $V = V_1 \parallel V_2$ is the variant from Figure 5.11.

The flow for data encryption working key generation is as follows:

1. The key, K, is XORed with the variant: $K' = K \oplus V$.

2. The result, K', is encrypted using itself in the TDES ECB mode to obtain the output key E: $E = Enc_{K'}(K')$.

3. The output of the encryption (two blocks) is the double-length TDES key for data encryption or MAC calculation.

Key Use	Variant 1	Variant 2
PIN Encryption	00 00 00 00 00 00 00 FF	00 00 00 00 00 00 00 FF
Message Authentication, request or both ways	00 00 00 00 00 00 FF 00	00 00 00 00 00 00 FF 00
Message Authentication, response	00 00 00 00 FF 00 00 00	00 00 00 00 FF 00 00 00
Data Encryption, request or both ways	00 00 00 00 00 FF 00 00	00 00 00 00 00 FF 00 00
Data Encryption, response	00 00 00 FF 00 00 00 00	00 00 00 FF 00 00 00 00

Figure 5.11: Worker key variants.

The AES DUKPT working key derivation algorithm follows the same steps as other AES DUKPT intermediate derived keys, with the only difference of having a different usage value in the Key usage indicator field.

Chapter 6

Regulation and Compliance

Payments are a highly regulated industry. Even in the field of cryptocurrencies, which lacks a central authority by design, regulators and law enforcement increase pressure on entities that deal with these instruments.

Depending on the entity type, it may be affected by financial authorities, central bank, privacy regulations, anti-money laundering laws, et cetera. In addition to various government agencies, the banking industry has its own rules and standards. Card schemes have thick rulebooks, too, and even if a payment service provider does not have a direct membership with a scheme, the rules – and the seasonal updates to these rules – will still apply.

The vast majority of the laws, guidelines, rules, and regulations apply to business processes, risk assessment, capital requirements, and other aspects of operations that do not relate to the technology directly.

A portion of rules affect technical integration: for example, updates to card scheme protocols may require changes in the transaction structure or the addition of a new field. Schemes place value on standard compliance; therefore, some rules require full adoption of a particular technical standard, such as EMV contact/contactless or EMV 3-D Secure.

Finally, explicit security and authentication requirements and guidelines sometimes translate into cryptographic algorithms and key management procedures or necessitate protocol adoption.

DOI: 10.1201/9781003371366-6

6.1 Payment Services Directive 2 (PSD2)

The Revised Payment Services Directive 2015/2366 (PSD2) [71], adopted in the pre-Brexit European Union, triggered several significant changes in the financial market.

The directive obliged banks to expose API access to bank accounts for information retrieval and payment initiation. It introduced a new class of regulated entities, the third-party processors (TPPs), and outlined three subtypes of service providers, depending on the services they were allowed to render to consumers.

Any bank under the EU jurisdiction was to allow any licensed TPP to connect to the bank's account access APIs without demanding a dedicated agreement. This requirement was implemented using TLS certificates and dedicated certificate authorities (see *Sections 4.1 Transport Layer Security (TLS)* and *1.11 Key Trust and Key Certificates*).

The directive had also introduced and defined the concept of *strong customer authentication (SCA)*. The SCA was defined as a process that involves at least two out of three possible authentication factors: knowledge ("something you know"), possession ("something you have"), and inherence ("something you are"), and it has to be applied to all payment transactions.

While the former measure focused on opening the banking ecosystem to new players, the SCA focused on combating fraud. The clarifying regulatory guidelines later listed several exceptions to the rule, but with PSD2 coming into force, most payment transactions involving EU entities had to undergo some form of strong customer authentication.

This regulatory change impacted card payments the most.

The response was twofold and differed for card-present and card-not-present environments.

Card schemes capitalized on the rollout of the EMV technology on the continent and relied on it to comply with the SCA mandate. Since the terminal already authenticated the card (see *3.4 Card Authentication*), the card constituted a possession factor. The PIN was a knowledge factor, and for payments where cardholder verification was happening on the consumer device (see *Section 3.4.3 Cardholder verification*), the devices used either a device PIN (also a knowledge factor) or biometrics (an inherence factor). Therefore, all necessary authentication factors were already in place in the card payment ecosystem, and the compliance was a relatively simple matter of adjusting the various amount and count thresholds on cards and terminals to ensure a PIN or consumer device-based CVM takes place as frequently as the law requires.

In the online world, the situation was much more challenging. Both the PAN and the CVV2 value were printed on the card. Consequently, possessing the card granted access to both these values and would not constitute two separate factors under PSD2. In order to support the mandate, schemes promoted the 3-D Secure 2.0 standard (see *Section 4.3 3D Secure and EMV 3-D Secure*). Since under the

3-D Secure protocol, the cardholder was to interact with the card issuer, the issuer then could authenticate the cardholder using an additional authentication factor, thus complying with the 2-factor authentication requirement.

Ironically, one of the drivers behind 3-D Secure 2.0 development was the need to significantly increase the percentage of frictionless flows in authenticated online interactions, encouraging all participants in the ecosystem to perform frictionless authentication as often as possible.

Due to the PSD2 law, the schemes simply moved the needle, making the frictionless flow the exception rather than the rule, and mandating the adoption of 3-D Secure 2.0.

While the majority of 3-D Secure 2.0 flows are secured using TLS (see *Section 4.3.4 TLS requirements*), the mobile app flows require additional application-level authentication using JOSE standards (see *Sections 4.3.5 Application-level security* and *4.2 JSON object signing and encryption (JOSE)*).

6.2   PCI SSC

In order to systemize security requirements for payment ecosystem participants, major card schemes have formed the Payment Card Industry Security Standards Council or PCI SSC.

The council publishes multiple security standards, which are freely available for all to access and use. Card schemes mandate certain levels of compliance with some of the standards. For example, compliance with the PCI Data Security Standard (PCI DSS) is mandatory.

In some cases, members of the card payments ecosystem can perform self-assessment of their compliance with particular standards. The Council publishes several self-assessment questionnaires (SAQs) covering various industry scenarios.

In other cases, a periodic independent audit by an approved assessor is usually required depending on the volume or importance of the entity.

If a particular entity does not interact with cardholder data or sensitive data, its systems are not within the scope of PCI standards.

In all other cases, for a service provider, the primary standard to comply with is the PCI Data Security Standard (PCI DSS), which covers the entire environment (physical and virtual).

For payment applications, there is the PCI Payment Application Data Security Standard (PCI PA DSS) which defines security requirements for payment applications.

For physical terminal devices, the PCI PIN Transaction Security Requirements (PCI PTS), PCI Software-based PIN Entry on COTS (SPoC), and PCI Contactless Payments on COTS (CPOC) apply, where COTS is a commercial off-the-shelf device. Acquirers and issuers also have to comply with the PCI PIN standard. Finally, the card-present environment may also comply with the PCI Point-to-Point Encryption (PCI P2PE) standard.

Usually, card schemes require full compliance with security standards. However, in some cases, they may grant a waiver for a particular kind of non-compliance. For instance, version 3.1 of the PCI PIN standard mandated transition to key block representation and exchange and specified a timeline for transition from TDES to AES pin block encryption (see *Chapter 5 Protecting the PIN*).

6.2.1 PCI PIN standard

The PCI PIN standard defines requirements for PIN data management, processing, and transmission. Other standards, such as PCI PTS or PCI P2PE, share key management principles with the PCI PIN standard.

Version 3.1 of the standard has 7 control objectives mapped into a hierarchy of detailed requirements. The control objectives themselves can be summarized as follows:

- PINs used in transactions are processed while ensuring they are kept secure.

- Cryptographic keys for PIN processing are created in a manner that makes guessing them not practically possible.

- Keys are transmitted, conveyed, loaded into HSMs and POS devices, managed, and administered securely.

- Equipment used to process PINs and keys is managed securely.

The standard elaborates on the control objectives, defining, for example, which certifications an HSM should possess to qualify as PCI PIN compliant, how the physical security of a key injection facility must be set up, and more.

The following are the standard requirements relevant to the topic of cryptography.

The standard lists three permitted methods for online PIN translation: fixed key, master/session, and DUKPT. Fixed keys in terminals are similar to fixed keys in host-to-host connections; see *Section 5.2 Zoning* for fixed keys management, *Section 3.4.3.5 Key management methods* for the master/session method description, and *Section 5.4 Derived Unique Key Per Transaction (DUKPT)* for the description of DUKPT.

The only approved algorithms for the online PIN encryption are TDES in ECB mode and AES. TDES is described in *Section 1.4.1 DES (DEA)*, ECB and other modes in *Section 1.8.1 Padding and cipher block chaining*, and AES can be found in *Section 1.4.2 AES*.

The online PIN must be encapsulated in a PIN block format 0, 1, 3, or 4 only, while the offline PIN must conform to PIN block format 2. The former are described in *Section 3.4.3.4 PIN block formats 0, 1, 3, and 4*, while the latter can be found in *Section 3.4.3.1 PIN block format 2 and offline plaintext validation*. The standard defines which PIN block formats may be translated into which during the PIN translation.

The standard describes key generation requirements. The keys are best generated using an HSM, i.e., a hardware solution. Other key generation methods are permitted but only if certified to comply with NIST SP 800-22 standard [72] and if not performed on a multi-purpose computing system. The key generation process must be organized in a way that will not allow compromise without collusion between trusted individuals.

Key conveyance is permitted only if the key is encrypted, transmitted as at least two separate components, conveyed using a key agreement algorithm, or shipped in a dedicated secure device. In the case of a public key (see *Section 1.5 Public Key Cryptography*), its integrity and authenticity must be protected by either a CA signature (see *Section 1.11 Key Trust and Key Certificates*), hash or MAC (see *Section 1.7 Hash Functions* and *Section 1.9 Message Authentication Codes*), or encryption.

If keys are conveyed under a key encryption key, there are requirements for the minimum size and the protocol allowed. If the key encryption protocol is TDES, it must be at least double length. A double or triple-length TDES key must not be encrypted with a key of lesser strength. TDES cannot be used to encrypt AES keys.

In the case of RSA (see *Section 1.5.1 RSA*), the key strength must be 80 bit (1024 bits for RSA), and at least 112-bit strength if the protected key itself is stronger than 80 bit, corresponding to 2048-bit RSA keys. POI devices must use 2048-bit RSA keys and SHA-2.

Recombination of key components must conform to a process where no bit of the resulting key can be determined without knowledge of all components. The recommended method is to XOR clear-text components. Key share mechanisms, such as Shamir's secret sharing (see *B.4 Shamir's Secret Sharing (SSS)*), are permitted if no custodian has access to more than two secret components.

If the keys are established using a key exchange method (see *Section 1.5.2 Diffie-Hellman key exchange (DHE)* and *Section 1.6.2 Elliptic curve Diffie-Hellman (ECDH)*), the minimum strength of the numbers used must be 2048 for Diffie-Hellman and 224 for elliptic curve Diffie-Hellman method.

The process of key injection into POS devices (see *Section 5.4 Derived Unique Key Per Transaction (DUKPT)*) is covered by a comprehensive set of requirements, addressing physical security, device, software, and processes of a compliant key injection facility.

The standard prescribes a key validation mechanism, key check value, as described in Key Exchange and Management. The standard also mandates the use of key blocks (see *Section 5.3.2 Key block*), allowing a transition period from the earlier methods (see *Section 5.3.1 X9.17 and variant formats*).

6.2.2 PCI PIN Transaction Security Standard (PTS), SPoC, and CPoC

The PCI PIN Transaction Security standard has requirements for Hardware Security Modules (HSMs) and for POS devices (which the standard calls points of interaction or POI).

The HSM part of the PTS standard (also known as PCI HSM) lists permitted functions and algorithms. In version 4 of the standard, the hash function list contains only SHA-2 and SHA-3 families, and symmetric algorithms are limited to AES and TDES with double or triple key length. For message authentication, CMAC, GMAC (GCM mode for signature only, see *Section 1.9.6 Galois/Counter mode*), and HMAC are allowed for AES. CMAC and CBC-MAC are allowed for TDES. Signature algorithms include DSA (see *Section 1.9.3 DSS (DSA)*), ECDSA (see *Section 1.9.4 ECDSA*), and RSA (see *Section 1.5.1 RSA*).

The key lengths align with the PCI PIN standard (see *Section 6.2.1 PCI PIN standard*).

The POI part of the PTS standard prescribes TDES of at least double-length keys and AES in either master/session or DUKPT modes (see *Section 5.4 Derived Unique Key Per Transaction (DUKPT)*). The keys for PIN encryption must not be used for other purposes, such as data encryption and authentication. This requirement is in line with the DUKPT algorithm.

The PCI Software-based PIN Entry on COTS (SPoC) standard defines requirements for a secure PIN entry on a commercial off-the-shelf device (COTS).

A traditional PED device has a display screen, a keyboard, and card reading interfaces (contact chip slot, contactless reader, and possibly a magnetic stripe reader). Such a device integrates hardware and software security measures to protect the encryption keys and the PIN entry from unauthorized access.

A SPoC-compliant solution consists of two modules: a COTS device with an application and a card reading device called *secure card reader – PIN (SCRP)*.

The COTS device is responsible for initiating the transaction with whatever user experience the designer of the solution envisions and for communication with the SCRP. Upon reading the card and establishing the desired CVM method, and if the desired CVM method is a flavor of PIN, the COTS device would also capture and encrypt the PIN, communicating it to the SCRP (see Figure 6.1).

The SCRP's responsibility is to re-encrypt the PIN, either for offline PIN validation (see *Section 3.4.3.2 Encrypted offline PIN*) or prepare an EPB for the COTS device to send to the payment network. In other words, while the COTS device is responsible for communication with the acquiring host, the data for that communication, including the online PIN block, is prepared by the card reader.

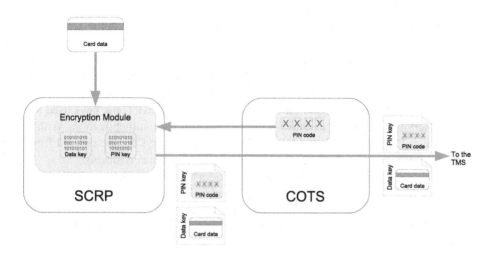

Figure 6.1: COTS and SCRP flow.

From the point of view of key management, the standard implies that the SCRP will undergo key injection as a more traditional POS in a dedicated key injection facility and will support a PCI PIN compliant PIN and encryption key management schemes. The SCRP and the application on the COTS device will use one of the approved algorithms with the approved key strength (see above the PCI HSM standard) to set up an encryption key to communicate the PIN from the COTS device to the SCRP.

The CPoC standard sets security requirements for solutions that allow contactless transactions on a COTS device. Unlike SPoC, there is no secure card reader involved. Consequently, a CPoC solution cannot process any PIN-based cardholder verification methods.

The cryptographic algorithms and the approved key strengths correspond to the PCI HSM standard.

6.3 PCI Point-to-Point Encryption (P2PE)

The PCI P2PE standard aims to secure a solution that will encrypt the data from the POS environment to the host, removing clear-text account data between these two points.

While the PIN blocks are secured using modern cryptographic methods (see *Chapter 5 Protecting the PIN*), other account data, such as the PAN, tracks 1 and 2, including CVV values, expiry date, and cardholder name (part of track 1), could be transmitted from the terminal to the host without violating existing security standards. The P2PE standard comes to patch this gap in the security of POS solutions.

The standard describes, at length, various security aspects of a secure environment. However, from the cryptography point of view, the approved algorithms and the valid key lengths align with the PCI HSM and the PCI PIN standards.

In particular, in the case of a method such as the DUKPT, the keys used for PIN encryption cannot be used for encryption and data authentication. With a compliant DUKPT solution, PIN and data encryption keys can be derived from the same intermediate key (see *Section 5.4.5 Working key derivation*).

However, in some existing solutions, vendors used two separate BDKs, deriving keys for PIN encryption from one derivation tree and keys for message encryption and authentication from another. While not necessarily more secure, this solution is more complex and wasteful. Still, it may be encountered in the field.

6.4   PCI DSS, PCI PA DSS, and PCI 3DS

The three standards, PCI Data Security Standard, PCI Payment Applications Data Security Standard, and PCI 3DS, put much demand on the architecture of a processing environment and its operation. However, the cryptographic aspect of these standards is

The standards are as follows.

6.4.1   PCI Data Security Standard (PCI DSS)

The PCI DSS standard describes requirements for the entire processing solution. The PCI DSS standard defines *cardholder data (CHD)* as the PAN, cardholder name, expiration date, and service code of the card. The standard defines *sensitive authentication data (SAD)* as the full track data, CVC/CVV, and PIN blocks. The environment which processes the CHD is called the *cardholder data environment (CDE)*, and systems that connect to it are called connected systems. While cardholder data can be stored (but must be protected), sensitive authentication data can only be stored temporarily for transmission purposes and cannot be kept persistently.

The PCI DSS standard describes security requirements for the network, the physical access to facilities, the endpoint security, and more. From the point of view of cryptography, the standard does not elaborate on acceptable methods or algorithm requirements. However, there are requirements for key rotation, where keys used to encrypt data are only used for a limited time and are replaced periodically. While not relating to the cryptographic algorithms themselves, this requirement usually impacts the design of the solution.

6.4.2 PCI Payment Application Data Security Standard (PCI PA DSS)

The PCI PA DSS standard governs the software developed for use in processing environments. There are not many demands that relate to cryptography in the standard. It bans SSL and earlier versions of TLS (see *Section 4.1 Transport Layer Security (TLS)*) and prescribes "strong cryptography" for the protection of sensitive data without going into further details.

An application that is compliant with PA DSS may not necessarily comply with PCI DSS once deployed. For example, such a compliant application may be deployed without proper network segmentation using firewalls, and while the application itself will follow the PA DSS standard, the solution as a whole will not. Therefore, each PCI PA DSS compliant application must have a PCI DSS implementation guide defining the method to deploy and configure the application in order for the result to be PCI DSS compliant, too.

6.4.3 PCI 3DS

The PCI 3DS standard came following the mandatory implementation of 3-D Secure 2.0 in Europe by the card schemes (see *Section 6.1 Payment Services Directive 2 (PSD2)*).

While the EMV 3-D Secure standard defines requirements for encryption of protocol messages, it is silent on security measures required on the Directory Server and ACS sides (see *Section 4.3 3D Secure and EMV 3-D Secure*). In a way, the PCI 3DS is to EMV 3DS as PCI DSS to PCI PA DSS.

The PCI 3DS standard contains many references to the EMV standard, including on the cryptography of the message exchange. In addition, it defines a detailed matrix of values that each party is permitted and not permitted to store. For example, the device information gathered by the mobile SDK can be stored by the DS and the ACS in an unencrypted form. However, it cannot be stored encrypted – thus making it harder for an attacker to gather ciphertext for a possible compromise of the encryption key.

The PCI 3DS standard, as its PCI DSS counterpart, also defines key rotation requirements for the cryptographic algorithms used as part of the 3-D Secure solution.

Appendix A

Bits and Digits

A.1 On XOR and One-Time Pad

Bitwise operations play an essential part in cryptography. Standard bit operations such as AND, OR, and XOR are available as built-in operators in many programming languages and therefore do not require additional implementation details in the context of this book.

Furthermore, more complex bit manipulations are part of some algorithms used in the payments domain, such as calculating parity bits or identifying the rightmost 1. While easy to implement straightforwardly, there are more efficient and somewhat spectacular ways to achieve the same result.

However, out of the entire range of bit operations, XOR stands out as being cryptographer's darling.

XOR or "exclusive OR" is an operation on bits that yields 1 if the bits differ and 0 if they are identical (see Figure A.1). It is denoted as "^" in the programming languages for this book and as $\oplus$ in formulas.

XOR has the following properties which make it such a handy building block for cryptographic algorithms:

- Any value, when XORed with itself, yields zero: $\forall a.\ a \oplus a = 0$.

- Any value, when XORed with zero, yields the value itself: $\forall a.\ a \oplus 0 = a$.

- It follows that any value, when XORed twice with another value, remains unchanged: $\forall a, b.\ a \oplus b \oplus b = a$.

DOI: 10.1201/9781003371366-A

$\oplus$	0	1
0	0	1
1	1	0

Figure A.1: XOR values.

Furthermore, XOR is a basic command in all modern processors, so its execution is fast on any system. Thus, XORing a value with a string of bits is an operation that is easily reversible and computationally cheap.

XOR can be used to implement, at least in theory, the only unbreakable encryption algorithm in existence - the *one-time pad*.

With the one-time pad encryption scheme, the sender generates a key and securely shares it with the receiver. The key must be as long as the sender's cleartext; the sender will only use the key once, hence the name - one-time pad. To encrypt the message, the sender XORs it with this sequence, and the receiver performs the same operation to decrypt it.

There is easy mathematical proof that the one-time pad algorithm is unbreakable, given that the key in use is truly random (also see section *1.10 Randomness and Key Derivation*).

Surprisingly enough, if the length of the key that is XORed with the cleartext is finite, it is pretty easy to break the encryption, knowing at least something about the nature of the cleartext (for instance, knowing that it is English).

The method goes as follows: if the attacker does not know the key length, it is possible to identify by repeatedly shifting the ciphertext by a varying number of bits and XORing it with itself, counting identical bytes. The percentage of identical bytes will be significantly higher when the shift is a multiple of the key length. It will be close to the index of coincidence in the English language.[1]

Knowing the key length, the attacker would then shift the ciphertext by the length of the key and XOR it with itself. As XORing a value with another value twice would yield the original value, this operation will cancel out the key and leave just the English text, XORed against its shifted self. From that point onwards, restoring the original text would be a straightforward exercise, so vividly described by Edgar Allan Poe in "The Gold Bug." [73]

A.2 Parity Bits

A parity bit is a simple yet efficient way to detect transmission errors: count 1-bits in a byte and set the parity bit so that the overall parity is always even (*even parity*) or always odd (*odd parity*).

---

[1] The index of coincidence is the probability of two letters randomly chosen from a text being identical.

For example, consider the 7-bit sequence of 0101110. It has four 1-bits, so if we work with even parity, the 8th bit will be 0, and with odd parity, 1.

The original DES algorithm used 64-bit or 8-byte keys but allocated each 8th bit for odd parity (see *1.4.1 DES (DEA)*). This design decision brought its keyspace down from 2^{64} to 2^{56}. However, specialized hardware's built-in validation of the key proved to be a useful way of detecting key transmission errors.

There are built-in methods in various platforms for parity calculation. For instance:

- odd parity flag for the low 8 bits of the machine word in Intel processors since 8008.

- even parity built-in function in the GCC compiler, *__builtin_parity*.

- ParityBit class in Java Card API.

- Integer.bitCount() and texttttBitSet.cardinality() methods in Java API (both return the number of 1-bits).

However, they are platform-specific and may require some typecasting.

The fastest method to obtain the parity bit value is a lookup table of 256 entries [74]. However, with a simple transformation of the original byte, it is possible to get a fast parity bit operation that uses a single 16-bit word as its lookup table.

Following is the C code for it, assuming the value is in the variable v and the parity bit is stored in the variable textttp:

```
size_t even_parity_8 (uint8_t v) {
size_t p;
/* Shorten the value of v to a nibble while preserving parity
*/ v ^=v>>4;
/* cut off the upper nibble as it is no longer needed */
v &= 0xf;
/* use the magic number 0x6996 as the lookup table
   with 16 entries */
p = (0x6996 >> v) &1;
return p;
}
```

Here, the idea is to XOR the first four bits of the value with the last four bits. The resulting nibble will contain a value from 0 to 15, which is used to search a lookup table (the value 0x6996) for the parity bit.

To understand why it works, consider that we XOR bits 7, 6, 5, and 4 with bits 3, 2, 1, and 0. This operation does not affect the overall parity: if only one of the corresponding bits is set, one bit will be set after the XOR. If neither or both

Value	Binary	Parity	Value	Binary	Parity
0	0000	0	8	1000	1
1	0001	1	9	1001	0
2	0010	1	10	1010	0
3	0011	0	11	1011	1
4	0100	1	12	1100	0
5	0101	0	13	1101	1
6	0110	0	14	1110	1
7	0111	1	15	1111	0

Figure A.2: Parity bit table.

corresponding bits are set, the result will contain zero, but removing two set bits will not affect the overall parity.

In code, we achieve this by shifting the value v right by 4 bits, XOR it with itself, then clearing the upper 4 bits using 0xf as the bitmask. The result is between 0 and 15 and has the same parity as the original value. The magic number of 0x6996 has bits of 0 and 1 in positions corresponding to the even parity of numbers from 0 to 15, and, therefore, shifting it right by this number and clearing all upper bits will yield the even parity bit (see figure A.2).

An example implementation of this algorithm in C is in src/bits.c, functions even_parity_8(), even_parity_16(), and even_parity_32().

A.3   Rightmost Bit (LSB)

Some applications, such as DUKPT (see section *5.4 Derived Unique Key Per Transaction (DUKPT)*), require finding the least significant or rightmost bit that is set to 1. This function is implemented in some platforms but under a slightly different name.

The position of the rightmost bit is identical to the number of the trailing zeros of the value. Therefore, for example, with GCC, there is a built-in function _builtin_ctz which returns the count of trailing zeroes.

However, this function is not present in other technology stacks and is, of course, not easily ported. Following is a simple but fast implementation [74] of finding the count of trailing zeros, shown here for 32-bit machine words:

```
size_t count_trailing_zero_bits_32 (uint32_t v) {
/* Turn v from xxxx1000 into 00001000 by using two's
   complement. */
v &= -v;
/* maximum of 32 zeroes for v==0*/
```

```
size_t c = 32;
/* if v is not zero, set all bits of c to 1 */
if (v) c--;
/* descend through the tree, unsetting bits of c if needed */
if (v & 0x0000FFFF) c -=16;
if (v & 0x00FF00FF) c -=8;
if (v & 0x0F0F0F0F) c -=4;
if (v & 0x33333333) c -=2;
if (v & 0x55555555) c -=1;
return c;
}
```

This method works by first isolating the rightmost set bit and then finding its exact position using a binary search tree.

The first step relies on two's complement representation of negative integers. Given an integer v, the value of -v is computed by flipping all bits of v and adding 1 to the result. We know that v has some bits set, followed by the rightmost set bit, followed by zero bits:

```
v  = xxxx1000
~v = XXXX0111
-v = ~v +1 = XXXX1000
```

When we negate v, all bits to the left of the rightmost set bit will flip. The rightmost set bit will become a 0, and all the trailing zeroes after it will be set to 1. Once we add 1 to the resulting value, it will not affect bits to the left of the rightmost bit, but all preceding 1s to its right will turn into 0 due to carry. Finally, the bit itself will flip to 1.

The resulting value will contain negated bits to the left of the rightmost significant bit and will be identical to the original value from that point onwards. If we now apply a logical AND, the operation will yield a value in which only the rightmost bit is set.

All that is left is to find its position. It can be done by iteratively shifting the value by one bit to the right until it is zero, but a faster method using a binary tree exists.

For brevity of the further explanation, assume that the input value is only one byte. We will only need three bits to store the result, as the worst case here is 7.

The variable v has a value in which only one bit is set. To find its exact position, we first initialize the counter to the maximum possible value, in this case, 8. We perform a boundary check - if the value is not zero, we subtract one from it. This step makes the value of c equal to 7 (binary 111).

We then apply the mask of 0x0F to the value. If the result is non-zero, the bit we seek is in the lower nibble of the source byte, and we should subtract 4 from c, setting it to binary 011. Otherwise, the value is in the upper nibble, and the most significant bit of c should remain 1.

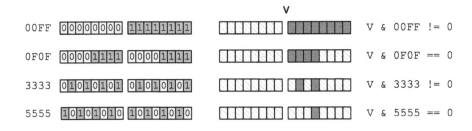

Figure A.3: Rightmost bit search.

Next, we check if the bit is set in the upper or the lower two bits of the nibble. For that, we use the mask of 0x33 (00110011). If the result is non-zero, the bit is in the lower two bits of the nibble, and the middle bit of c should be cleared (subtraction of 2 does exactly that).

Finally, we check if, out of the two-bit chunk to which c points, the sought-for bit is the least significant of the two. We do that with the mask of 0x55 (01010101). If the value is non-zero, the bit is in an even position, and we subtract 1 from c. See also Figure A.3 for an illustration.

An example implementation of this algorithm in C is in src/bits.c, functions count_trailing_zero_bits_8, count_trailing_zero_bits_16(), and count_trailing_zero_bits_32().

A.4 Leftmost Bit (MSB)

The DUKPT algorithm requires finding the most significant (the leftmost bit) set to one. The value can be calculated from the number of the leading zeroes. In GCC, there is a built-in function, __builtin_clz, which returns the count of the leading zeroes, which can then be used to calculate the rightmost bit position.

However, other stacks and even other compilers might not have it. Following is an implementation of finding the most significant bit in logarithmic time (5 iterations for a 32-bit input value) [74].

```
size_t log2_32(uint32_t v) {
const uint32_t b[] = {0x2, 0xC, 0xF0, 0xFF00, 0xFFFF0000};
const size_t S[] = {1, 2, 4, 8, 16};
int i;

size_t r = 0; // result of log2(v) will go here
for (i = 4; i >= 0; i--) {
if (v & b[i]) {
```

```
v >>= S[i];
r |= S[i];
}
}
return r;
}
```

The method works as follows. Two lookup tables are prepared. The tables contain bitmasks and the bit shifts which correspond to them.

The algorithm begins with the mask that covers the upper half of the input machine word. If the value is located in the upper 16 bits, the value of 16 is added to the result, and the input is shifted by these 16 bits to the right since the least significant 16 bits can now be safely discarded.

The process repeats for the mask of 0xFF00 and the shift value of 8. At this point, the rightmost bits of the input are guaranteed to be zero either due to bit shift or because no bit was set there initially. If the result of the AND operation is non-zero, there is a set bit in the upper byte. The value of 8 is added to the result, and the input is shifted right by 8.

The process continues for a sequence of masks and shift values of 4, 2, and 1, setting the relevant bit in the output and shifting the input accordingly.

An example implementation of this algorithm in C is in src/bits.c, functions `log2_8()`, `log2_16()`, and `log2_32()`.

A.5 Bit Cardinality

The DUKPT algorithm does not allow transaction counters with more than a fixed number of set bits. Therefore, whenever the next key serial number is computed (see *5.4.2 Key Serial Number (KSN)*), its bit cardinality must be calculated, and if it is over the limit, the value should be skipped.

The following simple loop quickly computes bit cardinality [74].

```
size_t bit_cardinality_8(uint8_t v) {
size_t c; // c accumulates the total bits set in v
for (c = 0; v; c++) {
v &= v - 1; // clear the least significant bit set
}
return c;
}
```

The method works as follows.

Imagine a binary number of form xxxxx1000, where 1 is the rightmost (least) significant bit. If we subtract 1 from this number, all bits to the left of the 1 will remain unchanged. The bit sequence from the least significant bit to the end of the value is 1000. After subtracting 1 from it, the value will become 0111. Applying the logical AND with the original value yields: xxxxx1000 & xxxxx0111 = xxxxx0000, clearing the least significant bit.

The procedure should continue until the value is zero; the counter c will accumulate the number of bits cleared by this operation.

A C implementation of this function can be found in src/bits.c, functions bit_cardinality_8(), bit_cardinality_16(), and bit_cardinality _32().

A.6 Luhn's Algorithm

Luhn's algorithm is a method to compute a check digit for a sequence of decimal digits [75]. It can detect an error in a single digit and most cases when two digits were swapped. Humans commonly make these mistakes during dictation or keying in long sequences of digits, making this algorithm very useful for card PANs.

The flow of the algorithm is:

1. The input sequence is scanned from right to left, and digits on odd positions are doubled (starting from the rightmost digit). For example, the sequence $3, 5, 7, 6$ becomes $3, 10, 7, 12$.

2. If the result of doubling a digit is greater than 9, the digit is replaced by the sum of its digits. In our case, $3, 10, 7, 12$ becomes $3, 1, 7, 3$.

3. The result is summed, and the remainder modulo 10 is calculated. In our case, $3 + 1 + 7 + 3 = 14 \equiv 4 \bmod 10$.

4. If the remainder is 0, the check digit is 0. Otherwise, the check digit is 10 minus the remainder, in our example, 6.

An example implementation of the algorithm can be found in src/bits.c, function luhn_check_digit().

A.7 Decimalization

In certain scenarios, such as with Track 1/Track 2 data, the medium uses an encoding that supports a limited character set. For instance, with the Track 2 data, the ANSI/ISO BCD data format only supports 16 characters, 10 of which are digits, and the rest are reserved as control characters.

The decimalization algorithm produces a sequence of decimal digits, usually of the length 3 or 4.

The algorithm scans the input byte vector, treating each nibble as a separate digit, from the most significant to the least significant. If a nibble contains a value between 0 and 9, i.e., a decimal digit, the digit is added to the output sequence. After the first scan, if not enough digits are found, the input vector is scanned again, subtracting 10 from each nibble.

For example, an input vector of 2A3B C4EF will yield 234 at the first pass. If the required sequence should be of four digits, during the second scan, A will get converted to 0, and the output will thus be 2340.

An example C implementation of the decimalization algorithm can be found in src/bits.c, function `decimalize_vector()`.

A.8   Base64 Encoding

Base64 encoding represents binary data with alphanumeric and special characters. The encoding (which is not an encryption algorithm!) converts an arbitrary binary value into a string that can be passed over a channel such as an email or as part of an HTTP parameter.

The principle of the encoding is simple:

1. The binary data is first padded with 0x00 bytes until the total length of the sequence is divisible by 3.

2. The data is converted into a string of 6-bit values (hence the name, $2^6 = 64$).

3. Each 6-bit value is mapped to a character according to the mapping table. The trailing zeroes appended to pad the value are encoded with a special padding character to separate them from trailing zeroes that are part of the original value.

The Base64 encoding has several flavors, the most widespread being the standard, the MIME, and the URL flavor [76, 77].

The MIME flavor uses the same set of characters as the standard and adds line breaks in the encoded value, thus allowing to embed a value (such as a picture or an attachment) in a mail message without impairing its readability on a non-supporting mail client.

The URL flavor is URL and filename-safe. For that purpose, it replaces the original characters of '+' and '/' with '-' and '_', correspondingly, and disallows any linebreaks or whitespaces.

As an example, take the ASCII string 'foob'. Its hexadecimal value is 0x666f 6f62, and it has to be padded with 2 zero bytes to the length of 6. The bit values of the result, split into chunks of 6, are as follows: 011001 100110 111101 101111 011000 100000 000000.

According to the mapping table, the output is Zm9vYg==.

The Base64 encoding is implemented in Python as part of the standard library module base64 and in Java as java.util.Base64.

An example of base64 URL encoding implementation in C can be found in src/bits.c, function base64url_encode().

Appendix B

Cryptographic Examples

B.1 Some Cryptographic Libraries

B.1.1 OpenSSL library

The C examples in this book and the source code repository use the OpenSSL 1.1.11 library. The distribution package and the installation instructions can be found on the project's official website, https://www.openssl.org [78]. Here we will cover some basics of the library to simplify understanding of the examples.

B.1.1.1 Input/Output

Input/output functions of the library work via BIO, the basic IO abstraction layer. In C, it is imported by including. To instantiate the basic data structure, one allocates a pointer to the BIO struct, and then uses one of the functions BIO_new_xxx().

For example, to allocate a basic IO structure that would point to a dynamic memory buffer, function BIO_new_mem_buf() is used. For a file descriptor, BIO_new_fd() is used. Functions also exist for accessing a file via FILE* structure and by file name; there are also functions for active and passive sockets.

These functions allocate memory, so BIO_free_all() or BIO_free() calls should be applied to free it up.

B.1.1.2 Memory management and error handling

As mentioned above, BIO functions all allocate memory for the structures they work with, and the caller needs to free the memory with the appropriate functions once it is no longer used or upon an error. In addition to standard memory management, the library supports secure heaps. A secure heap employs special facilities to protect the memory area from some buffer overrun exploits and is pinned to memory, so it is never swapped out to disk.

The library contains memory allocation functions that allow explicitly using the secure heap instead of the standard one.

The error handling is provided via err.h. The ERR_get_error() function returns the last error which occurred while invoking a library function, or zero if all operations were successful.

OPENSSL_cleanse should be used to cleanse local buffers that hold sensitive data such as keys.

B.1.1.3 OpenSSL 3.0 and EVP

In OpenSSL 3.0, the recommended cryptographic API has shifted from algorithm-specific functions, such as RSA_* or DH_*, to a high-level, consistent interface under EVP.

Instead of coding specific function calls, the EVP interface works with constants and function pointers, allowing, for instance, seamless migration from one block algorithm to another.

While for new implementations, the use of EVP is strongly recommended, we stick to the legacy OpenSSL 1.1.11 examples in this chapter since, as of now, OpenSSL 3.0 is relatively new and may not be available due to other constraints of a particular implementation.

B.1.2 Shamir's secret sharing scheme

Shamir's secret sharing scheme implementation, ssss, is available under the GNU GPL v2 license. The library can generate shares for a secret and reconstruct the secret given the shares. The library is available at http://point-at-infinity.org/ssss/ [79].

B.2 RSA

A quick recap of the algorithm:

The public key for the algorithm is a pair of two numbers, a product of two primes p and q, denoted as n, and a number e that is coprime with the least common multiple of $p - 1$ and $q - 1$, λ. The private key is the pair of two numbers, n and d, where the latter is a modular multiplicative inverse of e modulo λ.

The encryption of a message m is by raising m to the power of e modulo n. The decryption is by raising the encrypted message to the power of d modulo n.

To illustrate the RSA algorithm, we begin with two prime numbers, p and q.

Assuming $p = 43$ and $q = 67$, their product and the first part of our key, n, is 2881.

We calculate lambda as the least common multiple of $p - 1$ and $q - 1$, $\lambda = lcm(42,65)$. The resulting number, λ, is 462.

We now choose a number e that is coprime with 462. One such example is 145: its greatest common divisor with 462 is 1. e will be the second part of the public key.

To compute the second part of the private key, we need to find d such that $ed \equiv 1 \ mod \ \lambda$. Such d equals to 325, $145 \times 325 \equiv 1 \ mod \ 462$.

Now let us encrypt the answer to the great question of everything, $m = 42$, using the encryption key we have calculated.

$$m^e \ mod \ n \equiv 42^{145} \ mod \ 2881 = 1117 = c$$

To decrypt, we need to raise 1117 to the power of d modulo n.

$$c^d \ mod \ n \equiv 1117^{325} \ mod \ 2881 = 42$$

Now let us consider an actual example of key generation in C with OpenSSL.

As mentioned above, the public key is a pair of numbers n and e, and the private key is a pair of numbers n and d.

The number e is called the *public exponent*. To simplify and speed up calculations, the most frequently used public exponents are 3 and 65537 (the so-called first and fourth *Fermat primes*). The OpenSSL library contains two constants, RSA_3 and RSA_F4, correspondingly for these numbers.

The number n is called the *modulus*. The RSA key generation function of the OpenSSL library calculates it and d (the *private exponent*).

Following is an output for the public exponent of 3 and key size of 32 bit [8]:

```
RSA Private-Key: (32 bit)
modulus: 3107431477 (0xb937a435)
publicExponent: 3 (0x3)
privateExponent: 2071546611 (0x7b794af3)
prime1: 57803 (0xe1cb)
prime2: 53759 (0xd1ff)
exponent1: 38535 (0x9687)
exponent2: 35839 (0x8bff)
coefficient: 25371 (0x631b)
```

Assuming we are encrypting $m = 42$ with the public key, $m^e \ mod \ n = 42^3 \ mod \ 3107431477 = 74088 = c$.

For decryption, $c^d \ mod \ n = 74088^{2071546611} \ mod \ 3107431477 = 42 = m$.

An example of RSA implementation in C with the OpenSSL library can be found in test/test_crypto_primitives.c, function RSA_example(). Running the binary test_crypto_primitives will print out several test vectors for these algorithms. Note that the implementation generates new keys with each run, but the comments contain information on how to reuse key pairs.

B.3   Diffie-Hellman Key Exchange

A recap of the algorithm:

The sender and the receiver publicly agree on a prime number p and a primitive root g modulo p. The sender chooses a secret integer, a, and calculates the value of A. A is then sent to the receiver. The receiver chooses a secret integer, b, and calculates the value of B. B is then transmitted to the sender.

The sender calculates B^a, and the receiver calculates A^b. After completing these steps, they possess the same secret value, the shared secret key.

Assume $p = 43$. Let us assume $g = 5$, which is a primitive root modulo 43. The sender picks $a = 6$ as the secret number, and the receiver picks $b = 3$. The sender calculates:

$$A = g^a \ mod \ p = 5^6 \ mod \ 43 = 16$$

The receiver calculates:

$$B = g^b \ mod \ p = 5^3 \ mod \ 43 = 39$$

They exchange the values: the sender gets B and the receiver A.

Each party applies its corresponding secret number to the value they have received to calculate the secret key.

The sender calculates:

$$B^a \ mod \ p = 39^6 \ mod \ 43 = 11$$

The receiver calculates:

$$A^b \ mod \ p = 16^3 \ mod \ 43 = 11$$

Thus at this point, both parties have 11 as their shared secret, which can then be used to encrypt the actual message exchange.

Implementing the Diffie-Hellman would require two distinct steps: generating the domain parameters (the prime number p and the generator g) and generating a specific key. The former is lengthy and may have to be done in advance.

An example of Diffie-Hellman implementation in C with the OpenSSL library can be found in test/test_crypto_primitives.c, function DH_example(). Running the binary test_crypto_primitives will print out a test key exchange process for a small number of bits. Note that generation of the domain parameters can take hours for a large number of bits.

B.4 Shamir's Secret Sharing

Shamir's secret sharing implementation in C is available at `http://point-at-infinity.org/ssss/` [79]. Compiling it will yield two utilities, `ssss-split` and `ssss-combine`. The former prompts the user for a secret string, such as a password, and prints the requested shares.

For example, for the secret of a single ASCII letter A, the shares from one run are:

```
1-e5
2-f9
3-5b
4-d3
5-63
```

Combining any three shares out of the five above using `ssss-combine` yields the secret value.

B.5 DES and Triple DES

The DES and Triple DES algorithms have small input and output vectors, predictable key sizes, and straightforward implementation. With the OpenSSL library, DES encryption is easy to use.

The DES functions of OpenSSL use a `DES_cblock` input which is a byte array of 8 bytes. While it is possible to allocate it anywhere in the calling program, it is advised to do so within the secure heap (see *Section B.1.1.2 memory management and error handling*).

Rather than generate the key schedule for each encryption or decryption (see *1.4.1 DES (DEA)*), the OpenSSL library pre-generates it once using `DES_set_key()` and then reuses the schedule for subsequent encryption or decryption calls.

The `DSS_set_key()` function has two variants, `DES_set_key_checked()` and `DES_set_key_unchecked()`. If the checked version is used, the library will validate the key parity and check it against the list of weak and semi-weak keys.

Two and three separate key schedules need to be created accordingly for double- and triple-length keys.

Once a key schedule or schedules have been initialized, the encryption and decryption are handled using `DES_ecb_encrypt()`, `DES_ecb2_encrypt()`, and `DES_ecb3_encrypt()` functions. All three of them use DES in the EDE mode, and all three have a flag, enc, which can be set to `DES_ENCRYPT` for encryption or `DES_DECRYPT` for decryption.

An example of DES and TDES implementation in C with the OpenSSL library can be found in `test/test_crypto_primitives.c`, functions

DES_example() and TDES_example(). Running the binary test_crypto_primitives will print out several test vectors for these algorithms.

B.6 AES

The AES algorithm is easy to use with the OpenSSL library. Firstly, the AES_KEY structure has to be initialized by calling AES_set_encrypt_key() or AES_set_decrypt_key(). The functions get the number of bits in the key as an input parameter.

Unlike the DES, since there are no parity bits, no mismatching keys are possible with the AES algorithm.

Then, AES_ecb_encrypt() function does all the necessary encryption.

An example of DES and TDES implementation in C with the OpenSSL library can be found in test/test_crypto_primitives.c, function AES_example(). Running the binary test_crypto_primitives will print out several test vectors for the algorithm.

B.7 OAEP

The OpenSSL library contains functions to support OAEP. In particular, RSA_padding_add_PKCS1_OAEP() is a function that pads a value using the OAEP method. The RSA_encrypt() function can be told to apply OAEP transparently by using a padding parameter. In addition, the PKCS1_MGF1() function implements the MGF1.

Below is an example of such a computation with an empty label.

The padded data is: 0093 0761 BA8E 7139 D9E3 4B79 87D1 4ACC 1534 1C5A DAF1 D542 3655 1AFD E930 341F 6A54 C256 721E 0FA2 F68F 65CD 3777 891A A19E.

Here, we can already identify the first byte, 0x00. We know that the SHA-1 hash function was used. Hence, the following 20 bytes (93 0761 BA8E 7139 D9E3 4B79 87D1 4ACC 1534 1C5A DA) are the masked seed, and the rest is the seed for the mask of the masked seed. The remainder (byte sequence beginning from 0xF1 above) is fed into MGF1 to obtain a mask. The mask is applied to the 20-byte seed. The seed is fed into MGF1 again to obtain a mask. The mask is applied to the remainder of the data to obtain: DA39 A3EE 5E6B 4B0D 3255 BFEF 9560 1890 AFD8 0709 0000 0000 01DE ADBE EF. Here, the sequence 0xDA ... 0709 is a fixed hash value that is used whenever the label is empty, and the remainder is the zero padding, followed by 0x01, followed by 0xDEAD BEEF, the payload.

An example unwrapping of an OAEP padding in C with the OpenSSL library can be found in test/test_crypto_primitives.c, function OAEP_example().

Running the binary `test_crypto_primitives` will print a step-by-step recovery of a test array from the padding based on a random sequence.

B.8   DSS (DSA)

The preparation of the DSA process consists of two steps: defining the domain parameters (p, q, and g) and the actual key generation and sharing.

The domain parameters can be shared among many users, while the key pair's private key is kept safe with the sender.

An example of DSA implementation in C with the OpenSSL library can be found in `test/test_crypto_primitives.c`, function `DSA_example()`. Running the binary `test_crypto_primitives` will print out a test case of the algorithm. Note that with each run, a new k parameter will be generated. Therefore, the signature will differ with each run.

B.9   HMAC and CMAC

The HMAC and CMAC C examples with the OpenSSL library can be found in `test/test_crypto_primitives.c`, functions `HMAC_example()` and `CMAC_example()`, accordingly.

B.10   TLS Client

A basic TLS client implementation in C with the OpenSSL library can be found in `test/test_ssl.c`. The client connects to a certificate test server of a CA and requests its index page. The client also dumps the certificate it has retrieved from the server.

For troubleshooting a connection, the `SSL_CTX_set_verify()` call may be commented out; in that case, the client will continue to connect and will dump the certificate but will not validate it.

The client keeps its certificates in bin/data/cert.pem, a text file. For the client to recognize other certificates, their PEM form should simply be appended to that file. In most cases, both the intermediate and the root certificates will have to be present in the file for the validation to work against a real-life web server.

B.11   TLS Certificate Examples

The OpenSSL library contains comprehensive command-line tools for key generation, certificate manipulation, and more.

For example, let us consider creating an internal root CA and signing a server certificate with it.

In order to do so, the following steps are required:

1. Generate the root CA certificate and the root CA private key. The latter will have to be very well-protected.

2. Generate a server private key.

3. Generate a certificate request for the server.

4. Sign the certificate request using the root CA private key to obtain the server certificate.

5. Deploy the root CA certificate in the keystores of relevant clients and servers to enable automatic recognition of certificates it signs. In the example in TLS Client, the root CA should be added to the cert.pem file.

For the sake of the exercise, 512-bit RSA keys will be used. In production, at least 2048-bit strength is strongly recommended.

The OpenSSL framework supports password-protected storage. Its mechanism is simple: the passphrase is used to derive a unique key, without which it will be impossible to decipher the stored cryptographic materials. For this exercise, we will not use passphrases (−nodes flag will take care of that).

We will need the certificate subject. The canonical name (CN) will be "Test Root CA," the country (C) will be New Zealand, and the location (L) will be Taumatawhakatangihangakoauauotamateaturipukakapikimaungahoronukupokaiwhenuakitanatahu. The expiry date will be set to 356 days, and the hash function will be sha1. These settings correspond to the following command line:

```
openssl req -x509 -sha1 -days 365 -nodes -newkey rsa:512 -subj
  "/CN=Test Root CA/C=NZ/L=Taumatawhakatangihangakoauauotamate
aturipukakapikimaungahoronukupokaiwhenuakitanatahu"
  -keyout rootCA.key -out rootCA.crt
```

To view the certificate, we can use:

```
openssl x509 -n rootCA.crt -noout -text
```

This command can yield, for example:

```
Certificate:
    Data:
        Version: 3 (0x2)
        Serial Number:
            1f:bf:a6:91:12:de:4b:9d:9d:6b:4d:96:e8:b1:e6:d2:
26:ea:ca:0f
        Signature Algorithm: sha1WithRSAEncryption
```

```
        Issuer: CN = Test Root CA, C = NZ, L = Taumatawhakatangihan
gakoauauotamateaturipukakapikimaungahoronukupokaiwhenuakitanatahu
        Validity
            Not Before: Jul 21 17:20:31 2022 GMT
            Not After : Jul 21 17:20:31 2023 GMT
        Subject: CN = Test Root CA, C = NZ, L = Taumatawhakatangihan
gakoauauotamateaturipukakapikimaungahoronukupokaiwhenuakitanatahu
        Subject Public Key Info:
            Public Key Algorithm: rsaEncryption
                RSA Public-Key: (512 bit)
                Modulus:
                    00:c9:d6:d4:c6:27:99:22:e3:c6:e5:0f:8c:d1:b6:
                    31:35:55:12:bd:48:35:a3:f3:64:04:08:d2:0c:ac:
                    24:9e:56:19:e4:b8:28:44:80:fe:f3:46:3e:ae:9f:
                    58:93:30:ed:4d:34:57:f4:5c:ba:37:3e:17:f6:43:
                    8d:ab:e5:b9:a7
                Exponent: 65537 (0x10001)
        X509v3 extensions:
            X509v3 Subject Key Identifier:
                04:19:69:BA:50:93:F2:1B:4B:D9:6A:FB:BB:36:4A:8F:
1A:9C:5F:75

            X509v3 Authority Key Identifier:
                keyid:04:19:69:BA:50:93:F2:1B:4B:D9:6A:FB:BB:36:
4A:8F:1A:9C:5F:75


            X509v3 Basic Constraints: critical
                CA:TRUE
        Signature Algorithm: sha1WithRSAEncryption
            64:6f:5c:64:ed:aa:a5:94:dc:a8:75:8c:c8:53:96:83:77:8c:
            cc:18:5e:59:3a:c5:f2:dc:76:8d:09:be:e3:83:8f:dc:3d:48:
            d0:f8:4d:42:a7:3b:34:f3:fc:1c:bb:5f:b1:c8:3c:d7:53:0f:
            b3:78:63:a8:fb:76:72:08:5f:37
```

Then, we need the server private key. It is easily done by:

```
openssl genrsa -out server.key 512
```

For the certificate request, due to a large number of parameters, we should use a configuration file:

```
authorityKeyIdentifier=keyid,issuer
basicConstraints=CA:FALSE
keyUsage = digitalSignature, nonRepudiation, keyEncipherment,
dataEncipherment
subjectAltName = @alt_names

[alt_names]
DNS.1 = localhost.root
```

The command `openssl req -new -key server.key -out server.csr -config csr.conf` will generate the CSR.

To sign the CSR, the following command should be used:

```
openssl x509 -req -in server.csr -CA rootCA.crt  -CAkey rootCA.key
  -out server.crt -days 365 -sha1
```

The signed server certificate will be generated in server.crt.

These commands use weak hash functions and small bit sizes and skip multiple additional options that contribute to the solution's security. Therefore, they should be considered an illustration only.

Appendix C

EMV Examples

C.1 Issuer Certificate Generation and Public Key Recovery

An example of the issuer certificate generation can be seen below.

Below is the full issuer key. [1]

```
Issuer key: 00C1 17AD ED75 677D 4D74 5412 8417 45F6 CA48 E5C3
            7211 FB4C 7CA8 4957 47ED 183E 8A9F 3995 6FE3 54FF
            657D E2D4 6401 9BA3 1B2D 6F85 83D9 832A A802 8D8A
            75FF 8D63 4E92 CA6D 1A29 6205 585F 1127 1340 A537
            E93E B0EC D5B3 4109 FF8B FA1F 8C1E 0692 E489 B930
            9BCF 8E18 17D9 7D8D 074F 88D5 15C8 C1AE 8134 0596
            DB58 A901 D49E 23EC AEA7 3297 9BCD F3EF 5DCF 25BF
            867F FC08 F1C1 AAF8 83D4 6004 B467 6E53 4FC8 DE00
            2E20 B603 804F 2D73 41B2 D0C8 E176 C214 E446 A1E3
            766E 6E86 1B81 A93A C298 30CA 61
```

The issuer key length is shorter than the maximum and it is therefore padded with the value of 0xBB. With the mandatory header (in this case, the BIN is 0x4058 25) and the trailing exponent (0x03) the hash input would look like the following[2]:

---

[1] The leading zero byte is added to the key to indicate this is a positive value

[2] In case the public key is padded, the hash signature must include the padding.

DOI: 10.1201/9781003371366-C

Hash input: 0240 5825 FF10 2512 3445 0101 C101 00C1 17AD ED75
677D 4D74 5412 8417 45F6 CA48 E5C3 7211 FB4C 7CA8
4957 47ED 183E 8A9F 3995 6FE3 54FF 657D E2D4 6401
9BA3 1B2D 6F85 83D9 832A A802 8D8A 75FF 8D63 4E92
CA6D 1A29 6205 585F 1127 1340 A537 E93E B0EC D5B3
4109 FF8B FA1F 8C1E 0692 E489 B930 9BCF 8E18 17D9
7D8D 074F 88D5 15C8 C1AE 8134 0596 DB58 A901 D49E
23EC AEA7 3297 9BCD F3EF 5DCF 25BF 867F FC08 F1C1
AAF8 83D4 6004 B467 6E53 4FC8 DE00 2E20 B603 804F
2D73 41B2 D0C8 E176 C214 E446 A1E3 766E 6E86 1B81
A93A C298 30CA 61BB BBBB BBBB BBBB BBBB BBBB BBBB
BBBB BBBB BBBB 03

The hash output will be 8E00 3638 CEF0 F8D6 942C 0BE3 F25A E5E2 7E86 E9D3.

This value is appended to the full buffer (i.e., with the leading sentinel value of 0x6A) instead of the exponent to obtain the below input to the encryption algorithm:

Buffer: 6A02 4058 25FF 1025 1234 4501 01C1 0100 C117 ADED
7567 7D4D 7454 1284 1745 F6CA 48E5 C372 11FB 4C7C
A849 5747 ED18 3E8A 9F39 956F E354 FF65 7DE2 D464
019B A31B 2D6F 8583 D983 2AA8 028D 8A75 FF8D 634E
92CA 6D1A 2962 0558 5F11 2713 40A5 37E9 3EB0 ECD5
B341 09FF 8BFA 1F8C 1E06 92E4 89B9 309B CF8E 1817
D97D 8D07 4F88 D515 C8C1 AE81 3405 96DB 58A9 01D4
9E23 ECAE A732 979B CDF3 EF5D CF25 BF86 7FFC 08F1
C1AA F883 D460 04B4 676E 534F C8DE 002E 20B6 0380
4F2D 7341 B2D0 C8E1 76C2 14E4 46A1 E376 6E6E 861B
81A9 3AC2 9830 CA61 BBBB BBBB BBBB BBBB BBBB BBBB
BBBB BBBB BBBB BB8E 0036 38CE F0F8 D694 2C0B E3F2
5AE5 E27E 86E9 D3BC

Finally, the result is encrypted with the private key of the scheme to obtain the output:

Output certificate:
5C3F 1A47 55FF BC41 C4D6 139D 5270 6544 CABF D865
F80C 8EC7 389E 57A8 9545 2AF1 EBF1 1977 3397 E3ED
BEB2 4BAD 951F 43C8 0BA6 81D4 D944 E8FF 2831 5821
7468 2530 F416 0834 E1F7 D710 18AE 3F09 8724 414D
1968 3EC4 1C01 E92F 6CBA 9A9C 5D62 D333 ECA4 C827
320E 5D50 8D87 4E0A ABFB 8A92 6318 512F A30B A38F
7297 B24C 5C33 41AD BFD4 30F4 F59F A752 635C 7BE7
1F2E 6C60 6EFC 7B17 DB6A 71C1 64CC 4B40 461C 4391

```
B613 D93B BD98 0230 2027 BC6E 43A8 66D4 6C12 0A63
0E73 E0C5 B0F0 CA5B 0206 12ED 0DE3 367D D97C 3224
7B14 655B 6CB4 B15F 04DF F949 76BC 1589 8813 5B18
E103 42E9 CA02 9A3C 90B0 D875 F692 F1D7 BBBE C0AF
A317 B06A 061C 2952
```

The recovery of the issuer public key from the certificate can be seen below.
The certificate is deciphered using the scheme's public key to obtain the recovered raw data:

```
Recovered raw data: 6A02 4058 25FF 1025 1234 4501 01C1 0100 C117 ADED
                    7567 7D4D 7454 1284 1745 F6CA 48E5 C372 11FB 4C7C
                    A849 5747 ED18 3E8A 9F39 956F E354 FF65 7DE2 D464
                    019B A31B 2D6F 8583 D983 2AA8 028D 8A75 FF8D 634E
                    92CA 6D1A 2962 0558 5F11 2713 40A5 37E9 3EB0 ECD5
                    B341 09FF 8BFA 1F8C 1E06 92E4 89B9 309B CF8E 1817
                    D97D 8D07 4F88 D515 C8C1 AE81 3405 96DB 58A9 01D4
                    9E23 ECAE A732 979B CDF3 EF5D CF25 BF86 7FFC 08F1
                    C1AA F883 D460 04B4 676E 534F C8DE 002E 20B6 0380
                    4F2D 7341 B2D0 C8E1 76C2 14E4 46A1 E376 6E6E 861B
                    81A9 3AC2 9830 CA61 BBBB BBBB BBBB BBBB BBBB BBBB
                    BBBB BBBB BBBB BB8E 0036 38CE F0F8 D694 2C0B E3F2
                    5AE5 E27E 86E9 D3BC
```

Since the key is shorter than the maximum length and was padded, it doesn't
have to be combined with the remainder. The issuer key is therefore:

```
Combined key:       00C1 17AD ED75 677D 4D74 5412 8417 45F6 CA48 E5C3
                    7211 FB4C 7CA8 4957 47ED 183E 8A9F 3995 6FE3 54FF
                    657D E2D4 6401 9BA3 1B2D 6F85 83D9 832A A802 8D8A
                    75FF 8D63 4E92 CA6D 1A29 6205 585F 1127 1340 A537
                    E93E B0EC D5B3 4109 FF8B FA1F 8C1E 0692 E489 B930
                    9BCF 8E18 17D9 7D8D 074F 88D5 15C8 C1AE 8134 0596
                    DB58 A901 D49E 23EC AEA7 3297 9BCD F3EF 5DCF 25BF
                    867F FC08 F1C1 AAF8 83D4 6004 B467 6E53 4FC8 DE00
                    2E20 B603 804F 2D73 41B2 D0C8 E176 C214 E446 A1E3
                    766E 6E86 1B81 A93A C298 30CA 61
```

However, it is not sufficient to simply recover the value. It has to be validated
using the provided hash.

The input for the hash would be as above, containing the recovered raw data
from its second byte onwards with the public exponent appended to the padded
key instead of the hash signature:

```
Hash input:         0240 5825 FF10 2512 3445 0101 C101 00C1 17AD ED75
                    677D 4D74 5412 8417 45F6 CA48 E5C3 7211 FB4C 7CA8
                    4957 47ED 183E 8A9F 3995 6FE3 54FF 657D E2D4 6401
                    9BA3 1B2D 6F85 83D9 832A A802 8D8A 75FF 8D63 4E92
                    CA6D 1A29 6205 585F 1127 1340 A537 E93E B0EC D5B3
                    4109 FF8B FA1F 8C1E 0692 E489 B930 9BCF 8E18 17D9
```

```
7D8D 074F 88D5 15C8 C1AE 8134 0596 DB58 A901 D49E
23EC AEA7 3297 9BCD F3EF 5DCF 25BF 867F FC08 F1C1
AAF8 83D4 6004 B467 6E53 4FC8 DE00 2E20 B603 804F
2D73 41B2 D0C8 E176 C214 E446 A1E3 766E 6E86 1B81
A93A C298 30CA 61BB BBBB BBBB BBBB BBBB BBBB BBBB
BBBB BBBB BBBB 03
```

The key hash as computed would therefore be 8E00 3638 CEF0 F8D6 942C 0BE3 F25A E5E2 7E86 E9D3 which is equal to the value provided: 8E00 3638 CEF0 F8D6 942C 0BE3 F25A E5E2 7E86 E9D3.

The key is therefore valid and the recovered value is:

```
Recovered key:  00C1 17AD ED75 677D 4D74 5412 8417 45F6 CA48 E5C3
                7211 FB4C 7CA8 4957 47ED 183E 8A9F 3995 6FE3 54FF
                657D E2D4 6401 9BA3 1B2D 6F85 83D9 832A A802 8D8A
                75FF 8D63 4E92 CA6D 1A29 6205 585F 1127 1340 A537
                E93E B0EC D5B3 4109 FF8B FA1F 8C1E 0692 E489 B930
                9BCF 8E18 17D9 7D8D 074F 88D5 15C8 C1AE 8134 0596
                DB58 A901 D49E 23EC AEA7 3297 9BCD F3EF 5DCF 25BF
                867F FC08 F1C1 AAF8 83D4 6004 B467 6E53 4FC8 DE00
                2E20 B603 804F 2D73 41B2 D0C8 E176 C214 E446 A1E3
                766E 6E86 1B81 A93A C298 30CA 61
```

A C implementation of both methods can be found in src/emv.c, functions emv_sign_issuer_master_key() and emv_recover_issuer_master_key(). Running the example binary in bin/test_emv will print out this and other similar examples.

C.2 Static Data Authentication and AFL

The static data authentication is performed according to the following process:

1. The issuer public key is recovered (see *Section C.1 Issuer Certificate Generation and Public Key Recovery*).

2. The encrypted static authentication data value is decrypted using the issuer public key.

3. The result contains several header values, padding, and a hash value of the static data.

4. In order to validate the hash value, the terminal needs to prepare an additional data vector by collecting extra records as specified by the AFL.

Consider the following example of an AFL:

```
08 01 01 00
10 01 04 00
18 01 02 01
```

Name	Tag	Length	Value:
Template tag	0x70	0x10	
PAN	0x5A	0x08	4567 8901 2345 6789
Expiration date	0x5F24	0x03	3212 31

Figure C.1: Example of static data.

The first byte of each 4-byte sequence indicates the file, the second and the third bytes define the range of records to be read from the file, and the last, fourth, byte indicates how many records, starting from byte 2, should be used for the static data authentication.

The file number is contained in the five most significant bits of the first byte. In other words, values 0x08, 0x10, 0x18 (binary 00001000, 00010000, 00011000) correspond to files 1, 2, and 3. From the AFL example, we see that the overall data records are to be read as follows:

■ Record number 1 from file 1.

■ Records numbers 1 to 4 from file 2.

■ Records 1 and 2 from file 3, with the first record to be used for SDA.

According to the EMV standard, each file record has a nested tag-length-value structure, with the outmost tag being 0x70. This tag, in turn, contains individual data elements in the same TLV format. The rule for collecting data for the SDA is as follows:

1. Records from files 1 to 10 are concatenated without the outmost tag 0x70 and its length.

2. Records from files with file numbers over 10 are concatenated with tag 0x70.

In that case, the static data for authentication will be 5A08 4567 8901 2345 6789 5F24 0332 1231 (see Figure C.1).

A C example of SDA computation and validation can be found in src/emv.c, functions emv_validate_sda() and emv_sign_static_data(). Running the bin/test_emv file will print an example computation.

C.3 ICC Certificate Generation and Public Key Recovery

Assume that the PAN is 1234 5678 9012 3456 7890, the expiry date is 1230 and the certificate serial number is 1122 33. Let the ICC public key be:

```
00C7 B3F1 F50B B858 A2F6 BD3B EF32 6AC7 5701 1CDD
0EF9 C1B3 9811 4819 CDCC 933C AE1A D51F 6C1B 2A1F
612E 8663 CE39 D314 D3A2 FFB0 8772 DFA7 1A30 12A0
6BF5 57EF 9C18 FA75 D43F 055E 915A A03A 7C7A A2F2
73AB F699 C886 BFA4 8383 D19F 2E93 1F5A C96F 9844
80D1 EA91 DC03 3206 EF03 4D62 1097 CC0F F488 C81E
02C8 111D 26D0 8034 57
```

The hash function input would be:

```
0412 3456 7890 1234 5678 9012 3011 2233 0101 8101
00C7 B3F1 F50B B858 A2F6 BD3B EF32 6AC7 5701 1CDD
0EF9 C1B3 9811 4819 CDCC 933C AE1A D51F 6C1B 2A1F
612E 8663 CE39 D314 D3A2 FFB0 8772 DFA7 1A30 12A0
6BF5 57EF 9C18 FA75 D43F 055E 915A A03A 7C7A A2F2
73AB F699 C886 BFA4 8383 D19F 2E93 1F5A C96F 9844
80D1 EA91 DC03 3206 EF03 4D62 1097 CC0F F488 C81E
02C8 111D 26D0 8034 57BB BBBB BBBB BBBB BBBB BBBB
BBBB BBBB BBBB BBBB BBBB
```

Note that the issuer key is padded with 0xBB to the necessary length.

The hash output would be 8CE1 8199 1FA1 9CF9 F4D8 D079 54FC 7D66 2B32 47EC. The input to the encryption by the private key would consist of the start sentinel, 0x6A, the hash input, the hash output, and the end sentinel, 0xBC:

```
6A04 1234 5678 9012 3456 7890 1230 1122 3301 0181
0100 C7B3 F1F5 0BB8 58A2 F6BD 3BEF 326A C757 011C
DD0E F9C1 B398 1148 19CD CC93 3CAE 1AD5 1F6C 1B2A
1F61 2E86 63CE 39D3 14D3 A2FF B087 72DF A71A 3012
A06B F557 EF9C 18FA 75D4 3F05 5E91 5AA0 3A7C 7AA2
F273 ABF6 99C8 86BF A483 83D1 9F2E 931F 5AC9 6F98
4480 D1EA 91DC 0332 06EF 034D 6210 97CC 0FF4 88C8
1E02 C811 1D26 D080 3457 BBBB BBBB BBBB BBBB BBBB
BBBB BBBB BBBB BBBB BBBB BB8C E181 991F A19C F9F4
D8D0 7954 FC7D 662B 3247 ECBC
```

Encryption by the private key that corresponds to the above public key will yield the ICC certificate:

```
B727 A657 5F99 68B8 65B0 BF7B 47A1 8009 A31F E45B
55D4 D13E 0DAE E5AD 7AA6 FDC2 F5A2 8C2C 2EDD 1416
1B1D 6794 3531 27EA 5BEE CAF2 6EFF B6C5 C3BD 0A1F
041B D7EA 1625 4CD8 7B6E EAA4 E8D3 4F0C EB52 A13A
8FD2 F9E8 90E4 A400 FFF8 EEED 29A5 13CB FEEB BB03
```

```
FCBE 1181 8417 3F1D FD65 4296 5C09 C5BC 3291 EB75
19BA 5F1D 000D D9C7 DF4B EF74 F236 6067 77C4 9042
FE8E 93F9 2CC3 F102 ED5D 0C4E 6878 FA75 CC95 52FA
43CC CDBA B025 4303 C0E1 5C8C EDA4 3709 3C96 13CA
7B14 C94E 0169 F7A0 8C79 0D79
```

The key recovery process would work as follows: the certificate is decrypted with the issuer public key to yield:

```
6A04 1234 5678 9012 3456 7890 1230 1122 3301 0181
0100 C7B3 F1F5 0BB8 58A2 F6BD 3BEF 326A C757 011C
DD0E F9C1 B398 1148 19CD CC93 3CAE 1AD5 1F6C 1B2A
1F61 2E86 63CE 39D3 14D3 A2FF B087 72DF A71A 3012
A06B F557 EF9C 18FA 75D4 3F05 5E91 5AA0 3A7C 7AA2
F273 ABF6 99C8 86BF A483 83D1 9F2E 931F 5AC9 6F98
4480 D1EA 91DC 0332 06EF 034D 6210 97CC 0FF4 88C8
1E02 C811 1D26 D080 3457 BBBB BBBB BBBB BBBB BBBB
BBBB BBBB BBBB BBBB BBBB BB8C E181 991F A19C F9F4
D8D0 7954 FC7D 662B 3247 ECBC
```

While the public key is already visible in the decrypted value, starting with the C7B3 F1F5 sequence, its authenticity still needs to be confirmed.

For that, the hash value at the end of the decrypted array is truncated and the public exponent is appended instead:

```
0412 3456 7890 1234 5678 9012 3011 2233 0101 8101
00C7 B3F1 F50B B858 A2F6 BD3B EF32 6AC7 5701 1CDD
0EF9 C1B3 9811 4819 CDCC 933C AE1A D51F 6C1B 2A1F
612E 8663 CE39 D314 D3A2 FFB0 8772 DFA7 1A30 12A0
6BF5 57EF 9C18 FA75 D43F 055E 915A A03A 7C7A A2F2
73AB F699 C886 BFA4 8383 D19F 2E93 1F5A C96F 9844
80D1 EA91 DC03 3206 EF03 4D62 1097 CC0F F488 C81E
02C8 111D 26D0 8034 57BB BBBB BBBB BBBB BBBB BBBB
BBBB BBBB BBBB BBBB BBBB
```

Hashing this value with the SHA-1 yields 8CE1 8199 1FA1 9CF9 F4D8 D079 54FC 7D66 2B32 47EC, which is identical to the value provided in the decrypted certificate.

The ICC public key certificate contains the hash value of data provided in the certificate and the static data used for the static data authentication (see *Sections 3.4.1 Static data authentication* and *C.2 Static Data Authentication and AFL*).

C.4   Dynamic Signature Generation

For the dynamic signature generations, let us assume FEEB DAED as the ICC dynamic data value, and DEAD BEEF as the terminal dynamic data.

The input for the hash function would therefore be:

```
0501 04FE EBDA EDBB BBBB BBBB BBBB BBBB BBBB BBBB
BBBB BBBB BBBB BBBB BBBB BBBB BBBB BBBB BBBB BBBB
BBBB BBBB BBBB BBBB BBBB BBBB BBBB BBBB BBBB BBBB
BBBB BBBB BBBB BBBB BBBB BBBB BBBB BBBB BBBB BBBB
BBBB BBBB BBBB BBBB BBBB BBBB BBBB BBBB BBBB BBBB
BBBB BBBB BBBB DEAD BEEF
```

Hashing of the above value would yield A102 7643 7398 D028 4A99 9E2D 9841 D560 D1F7 DCCA. This value is appended to the hash function input and, together with the start and end sentinels, the input to the encryption by the ICC private key would be:

```
6A05 0104 FEEB DAED BBBB BBBB BBBB BBBB BBBB BBBB
BBBB BBBB BBBB BBBB BBBB BBBB BBBB BBBB BBBB BBBB
BBBB BBBB BBBB BBBB BBBB BBBB BBBB BBBB BBBB BBBB
BBBB BBBB BBBB BBBB BBBB BBBB BBBB BBBB BBBB BBBB
BBBB BBBB BBBB BBBB BBBB BBBB BBBB BBBB BBBB BBBB
BBBB BBBB BBBB BBA1 0276 4373 98D0 284A 999E 2D98
41D5 60D1 F7DC CABC
```

The encryption would then yield:

```
8F7F 56F5 6786 4C0F 4B44 BFE8 6D68 306A AD3F F4C7
FA20 9565 D970 2B9A B6D7 E46E 5E4D 5856 C455 81FF
F888 F7AE A7F3 2BB0 960B 1559 D763 1272 1672 FD33
BF1D 3DF8 6378 8679 6DFA CBAA 936B D45E C963 27DF
7B24 2079 1320 ED89 70A9 1677 EF86 C0F8 E078 0A8C
AD0D E4A9 7491 0607 C5E3 41A1 FA43 05E8 2B72 896A
A3A4 AEE7 5FCF 471E
```

A C example of DDA computation and validation can be found in src/emv.c, functions emv_validate_dda() and emv_sign_dynamic_data(). Running the bin/test_emv file will print an example computation.

C.5   ICC Master Key Derivation

C.5.1   Option A

Option A is relevant for the TDES algorithm and PANs shorter than or equal to 16 digits. A quick recap of the algorithm:

1. The sequence number (CSN) is appended to the PAN.

2. The result is right-padded with zeros if its length is less than 8 bytes.

3. The rightmost 8 bytes of the result is the sought Y.

4. The value of Y is encrypted with TDES using IMK as the key to obtain the left half of the key.

5. The value of Y is negated by applying either bitwise NOT or XOR with the mask of 0xFF.

6. The outcome of Step 5 is encrypted with TDES using IMK as the key to obtain the right half of the key.

7. The left and the right halves are concatenated, and parity bits are corrected in the outcome to form a valid TDES key.

Let us assume the PAN value of 9012 3454 3210 1232 and the CSN of 01. The Issuer Master Key (IMK) is DFAD BFEF 0123 4567 8986 6443 DFAD BFEF. Then, the algorithm state is as follows:

1. The internal buffer value is 9012 3454 3210 1232 01, which the CSN appended to the PAN.

2. The length of the result is more than 8 bytes, so the rightmost 8 bytes are taken to obtain the value of $Y = 1234\ 5432\ 1012\ 3201$.

3. The value is encrypted using triple DES encryption in the ECB mode with the IMK to obtain 148C 5F5F D894 7763.

4. The value, Y, is negated to obtain EDCB ABCD EFED CDFE.

5. The result is encrypted with the same IMK to obtain 6664 15FD A58B 677C.

6. The left and right halves, concatenated, yield 148C 5F5F D894 7763 6664 15FD A58B 677C, which after the parity bit correction becomes 158C 5E5E D994 7662 6764 15FD A48A 677C.

C.5.2   Option B

Option B is relevant for the TDES algorithm and PANs longer than 16 digits. It essentially adds a shortening phase that maps the PAN and the CSN into a 16-digit value.

A quick recap of the algorithm:

1. The sequence number (CSN) is appended to the PAN.

2. If the total number of nibbles is odd, the result is left-padded with a single zero.

3. The result is hashed using SHA-1 to obtain a 20-byte hash value.

4. The output of the hash is decimalized to obtain a 16-digit value.

5. The steps of the Option A algorithm are applied to the outcome.

Let us assume the PAN value of 9876 5432 1012 3456 789 (19 digits) and the CSN of 01.

1. The input vector after the concatenation and the alignment will contain 0987 6543 2101 2345 6789 0100.

2. Its SHA-1 hash digest will be FBC4 FDF0 2B0E F7F0 801D 8C0D 02DD 609D 8BEA D233.

3. Decimalization of this value yields 4020 7080 1800 2609. This value is used as the input to the process described above under Option A.

4. The output of the process yields the key value of E5AB 98AB 5E76 F757 FEDC 7F01 6E5E 2358.

C.5.3   Option C

Option C is relevant for the AES algorithm and PANs of any length. The key derivation algorithm is as follows:

1. The sequence number (CSN) is appended to the PAN.

2. The result is left-padded with zeroes to the full length of 16 bytes to obtain Y.

3. The output is encrypted with the provided key: $R_1 = E_K(Y)$.

4. If the desired key length is larger than the AES block size, the value Y is inversed: $Y' = Y \oplus$ FFFF FFFF FFFF FFFF FFFF FFFF FFFF FFFF.

5. Y' is encrypted to obtain $R_2 : R_2 = E_K(Y')$.

6. The necessary number of bytes is used from $R_1 \parallel R_2$ to obtain the desired result.

Assuming the PAN value of 9012 3454 3210 1232, the CSN of 01, and the AES key $K =$ DFAD BFEF 0123 4567 8986 6443 DFAD BFEF, let the desired key length be 192 bits. Then, the process is as follows:

1. The input vector is $Y = $ 0000 0000 0000 0090 1234 5432 10123201.

2. The output of this value's encryption using AES with the key K, R_1, is as follows: $R_1 =$ 3AD9 5FE6 AD75 062D FCF1 9D83 4504 AC23.

3. Since the output is 128 bits long and the required key length is 192, the process continues. The inverted input vector, $Y' =$ FFFF FFFF FFFF FF6F EDCB ABCD EFED CDFE.

4. Its encryption result using AES with the key K is 7A49 8222 9225 7A16 F2B7 6168 B4E2 B574. Out of this result, only the first 8 bytes are used.

5. The end result is 3AD9 5FE6 AD75 062D FCF1 9D83 4504 AC23 7A49 8222 9225 7A16.

An example C implementation of the process can be found in `src/emv.c`, function `emv_derive_icc_master_key()`.

C.6 ICC Session Key Derivation

The long version of the session key derivation has the following key steps:

1. The card appends the value of 0xF0 to the ATC value and zero-pads the result to the full length of the input block.

2. The card encrypts the result to obtain the first part of the session key.

3. Next, the card appends the value of 0x0F to the ATC and zero-pads the result to the full length of the input block.

4. The card encrypts the result to obtain the second part of the session key.

Let us assume that the ICC Master Key is obtained using the process above (see *Section C.3 ICC Certificate Generation and Public Key Recovery*), and it is the TDES double-length key 158C 5E5E D994 7662 6764 15FD A48A 677C, and that the ATC is 0001.

1. The value of ATC with the 0xF0 appended yields 0001 F000 0000 0000.

2. After encryption, the first half of the session key is B027 E58F 2D55 6547.

3. The value of ATC with the 0x0F appended yields 0001 0F00 0000 0000.

4. After encryption, the second half of the session key is ABA7 1B83 E6EC 4495.

5. The combined output is B027 E58F 2D55 6547 ABA7 1B83 E6EC 4495, which after fixing the parity bit yields B026 E58F 2C54 6446 ABA7 1A83 E6EC 4594.

A C implementation of the process can be found in `src/emv.c`, function `emv_derive_icc_session_key()`.

C.7 ARQC Generation

The recommended algorithm for ARQC generation with TDES is as follows:

1. The value of 0x80 is appended to the data.

2. The result is padded so that its length is a multiple of 8 bytes and is split into 8-byte chunks.

3. The key is split into two halves, K_1 and K_2.

4. The data is encrypted with the single DES algorithm in the CBC mode (*Section 1.8.1 Padding and cipher block chaining*) using the session key's first half and a zero initialization vector. In other words, for each chunk, the output of the previous round is XORed with the chunk and then fed into the next round.

5. The result is decrypted using the second half of the session key.

6. The result is encrypted again using the first half of the session key.

7. The outcome is the ARQC.

With the AES, the ARQC value is the CMAC of the data (see *Section B.9 HMAC and CMAC*).

Let us assume the session key derived using one of the provided examples (see *Section C.6 ICC Session Key Derivation*), B026 E58F 2C54 6446 ABA7 1A83 E6EC 4594, and let the input data be the following 25-byte sequence: 0000 0000 0840 0000 0000 0008 4018 1200 0106 0112 0300 0000 00.

1. The value of 0x80 is appended to the data which turns into 0000 0000 0840 0000 0000 0008 4018 1200 0106 0112 0300 0000 0080.

2. Since the length of the result is now 26, it needs to be padded to the length of 32 by adding zeroes and split into 8-byte chunks: 0000000008400000, 0000000840181200, 0106011203000000, 0080000000000000.

3. The data is encrypted with a zero IV using CBC and K as the key.

4. The result is 9635 5B7C 0010 05F7 which is the ARQC.

An example C implementation of the process can be found in src/emv.c, emv_generate_arqc() function.

C.8 ARPC Generation

The EMV standard describes two methods for the generation of the ARPC value. With Method 1, the incoming ARQC is XORed with the 2-byte authorization response code and then encrypted with the session key. With Method 2, the ARQC, the card status update (CSU), and the Proprietary Authentication Data are concatenated and fed into a signature algorithm described in ARQC Generation.

Consider the aforementioned example in which the key, B026 E58F 2C54 6446 ABA7 1A83 E6EC 4594, yields the ARQC, 9635 5B7C 0010 05F7. Let the ARC be 0001. In that case, to generate the ARPC, the issuer:

1. XORs the ARC with the ARQC, obtaining 9634 5B7C 0010 05F7.

2. Encrypts the result with the session key.

3. The output, 8453 5883 EAC6 557A, is the ARPC.

An example C implementation of the process can be found in src/emv.c, emv_generate_arpc() function.

Appendix D

PIN Examples

D.1 PIN Block Formats

PIN block formats 0, 1, 2, and 3 differ from format 4 in at least two ways. Besides being twice the length, format 4 PIN block is encrypted with AES in the CBC mode, formats 1 and 2 have a single block encrypted with TDES in the ECB mode, and formats 0 and 3 XOR the PIN data with the PAN data prior to encryption.

Assume that the PIN is 12345 and the PAN is 123456789012345.

Format 0 PIN block would be a result of XORing two input blocks.

The first would be 0512 345F FFFF FFFF, where the format (0), the PIN length (5), and the PIN itself are padded with 0xF to the full block length.

The second block is 0000 3456 7890 1234, where the last 12 digits of the PAN without the check digit are placed in the last 12 nibbles of the block.

The final PIN block will be an XOR of these two values or 0512 0009 876F EDCB.

Format 1 PIN block is used when no PAN is available, but it may contain a unique ID of some form after the PIN value. The PIN value is padded with random bytes if no unique ID is available. For the data above, the format 1 PIN block would look like 1512 345R RRRR RRRR, where R denotes a random value.

Format 2 PIN block is used in EMV offline PIN authentication. It has the format of the first block of the format 0 PIN block, i.e., format, length, PIN followed by 0xF padding: 2512 345F FFFF FFFF.

DOI: 10.1201/9781003371366-D

Format 3 PIN block differs from format 0 in that it uses random padding instead of the 0xF constant. For the example above, the first block of format 3 will contain 3512 345R RRRR RRRR, the second block will contain 0000 3456 7890 1234, and the final output will be the XOR of these two values.

The encryption and decryption of these PIN block formats are performed with TDES in the ECB mode.

Format 4 PIN block would be obtained via a more complex procedure. First, the two input blocks, I_1 and I_2, are formed as follows:

1. I_1 contains the format indication, PIN, and padding of 0xA to 8 bytes, followed by 8 random bytes. For the example above, $I_1 = $ 4512 345A AAAA AAAA RRRR RRRR RRRR RRRR.

2. I_2 contains the length of PAN minus 12 as the first nibble, followed by the zero-padded PAN: $I_2 = $ 4012 3456 7890 1234 5000 0000 0000 0000. Since the PAN has 16 digits, the first nibble is $16 - 12 = 4$.

The encryption of the PIN block is done using AES in CBC mode with a zero IV. In other words, assuming the key is K:

$$C_1 = E_K(I_1)$$

$$C_2 = E_K(I_2 \oplus C_1)$$

The result, C_2, is the PIN block. Its decryption process is also AES in the CBC mode, but it works as follows: assuming that C_2 is the ciphertext above, I_2 is reconstructed from the PAN and is appended to C_2 as the second block of the ciphertext. CBC decryption is then performed. The reason it works is below:

1. I_2 is constructed from the known data.

2. The PIN block is decrypted using K to obtain $M_1 = D_K(C_2) = D_K(E_K(I_2 \oplus C_1)) = I_2 \oplus C_1$.

3. The result is XORed with I_2: $M_2 = M_1 \oplus I_2 = I_2 \oplus C_1 \oplus I_2 = C_1$.

4. The result is decrypted using K again: $D_K(C_1) = D_K(E_K(I_1)) = I_1$.

An example C implementation of PIN block formatting can be found in src/pin.c, function make_pin_block(). Running bin/test_pin will print out several test examples of PIN blocks in various formats.

An example C implementation of PIN block format 4 encryption and decryption can be found in src/pin.c, functions encrypt_format_4_block() and decrypt_format_4_block(). The aforementioned test_pin binary will also print out a test example of format 4 encryption and decryption.

D.2 Variant Key Encryption

A typical variant key encryption scheme involves applying a single mask byte to a part of the key encryption key depending on the chunk of the key being encrypted. As an HSM typically performs these operations, its manufacturer would specify a couple or a triplet of byte variants to be applied to a specific portion of the KEK before encrypting each of the respectful key parts.

In the example implementation, the byte mask is applied to the first byte of the second half of the key encryption key. Thus, if the variants are 0xA6 and 0xED, and the KEK is FFFF FFFF FFFF FFFF FFFF FFFF FFFF FFFF, the first half of the key will be encrypted with FFFF FFFF FFFF FFFF 59FF FFFF FFFF FFFF and the second with FFFF FFFF FFFF FFFF 12FF FFFF FFFF FFFF.

An example C implementation of variant encryption can be found in src/pin.c, function encrypt_key_variant(). Running the bin/test_pin binary will print a couple of examples of its operation.

D.3 Key Block Key Derivation

There are two key block working key derivation methods, variant-based and binding, the latter using a standard-compliant derivation mechanism.

With the variant derivation method, the key block protection key is XOR'ed with a mask, 'E' (0x45) for encryption and 'M' (0x4D) for MAC.

The ANSI TR-31 standard [68] contains examples of each method. A C implementation of the variant method can be found in src/tr31.c, in the tr31_derive_variant() function.

With the binding key derivation method, a value with a counter is fed into the CMAC function with the KBPK as the key until the required number of bytes is generated.

Consider the following example. Assume that the key block protection key is 1D22 BF32 387C 600A D97F 9B97 A513 11AC, and the binding method is used to derive a double-length TDES encryption key using TDES. In that case, the base value for the key derivation will be:

01 (counter) 0000 (key usage - encryption) 00 (separator) 0000 (2TDES algorithm) 0080 (16 bytes key length).

TDES encryption of 0100 0000 0000 0080 using the aforementioned key will yield BCE8 E2AD 5D44 89FD. The next block will have the value of 02 in the counter byte. TDES encryption of 0200 0000 0000 0080 will yield 0EA5 236A 884D AC58; therefore, the full key output will be BCE8 E2AD 5D44 89FD 0EA5 236A 884D AC58.

A C implementation of the variant method can be found in src/tr31.c, in the tr31_derive_binding() function. Running the binary bin/test_tr31 will print this and other variant and binding method derivation examples.

D.4 TDES DUKPT

D.4.1 Initial key derivation

Assume that the BDK is DEAD BEEF 2233 4455 DEAD BEEF 2233 4455, and the initial KSN is FFFF DEAD BEEF 2233 4000.

The Initial Key is derived from the BDK using the following steps:

1. The leftmost 8 bytes of the KSN are encrypted with TDES using the BDK as the key, yielding C133 69A4 8710 4C04.

2. The BDK is XORed with the variant, C0C0 C0C0 0000 0000 C0C0 C0C0 0000 0000, yielding 1E6D 7E2F 2233 4455 1E6D 7E2F 2233 4455.

3. The leftmost bytes of the KSN are encrypted with TDES using the modified BDK as the key, yielding 5E0D 0D55 C294 D609.

4. The two intermediate results are concatenated to yield C133 69A4 8710 4C04 5E0D 0D55 C294 D609, the initial key.

D.4.2 Intermediate key derivation

The intermediate key derivation of the TDES DUKPT standard attempts to utilize a relatively short KSN as the source of entropy while also trying to leverage the full 128 bits of the key for encryption (as opposed to the 112 bits that the standard TDES algorithm actually uses due to the parity bits).

The derivation process utilizes a "crypto register," consisting of two 8-byte halves, and stores the intermediate and the outcome of the derivation process.

Assume we are using the initial key above, its left half is $K_1 = $ C13369A487104C04, and its right half is $K_2 = $ 5E0D0D55C294D609. Let the KSN be FFFF DEAD BEEF 2220 0001. For this value of the transaction counter part of the KSN (1), the derivation process is done directly from the initial key.

The process commences as follows:

1. The rightmost 64 bits of the KSN, DEAD BEEF 2220 0001, are XORed with K_2, yielding $C_2 = KSN \oplus K_2 = $ 80A0B3BAE0B4D608.

2. The result is DES-encrypted using K_1: $C_2 = E_{K_1}(C_2) = $ D765A3944910027A.

3. The result is XORed with K_2 again, $C_2 = C_2 \oplus K_2 = $ 8968AEC18B84D473, yielding the second half of the output key.

4. The key K is XORed with the variant, C0C0 C0C0 0000 0000 C0C0 C0C0 0000 0000 to obtain $K' = K'_1 \parallel K'_2 = $ 01F3A96487104C049ECDCD95C294D609.

5. The process is repeated for the first half. The KSN is XORed with K_2':
$C_1 = C_1 \oplus K_2' = $ 4060737AE0B4D608.

6. The result is encrypted using K_1'. $C_1 = E_{K_1}'(C_1) = $ 1F228F640CF50AB0.

7. C_1 is once again XORed with K_2': $C_1 = C_1 \oplus K_2' = $ 81EF42F1CE61DCB9.

The intermediate key for the KSN of FFFF DEAD BEEF 2220 0001 is, therefore, $C_1 \parallel C_2 = $ 81EF42F1CE61DCB98968AEC18B84D473.

Now assume the KSN in question is KSN: FFFF DEAD BEEF 0100 200B. The least significant bits of it are 1011. According to the derivation process, the value will be derived as follows:

1. The key corresponding to the KSN with the trailing bits of 1000 (0x08) is derived from the initial key. For the example above (initial key of C133 69A4 8710 4C04 5E0D 0D55 C294 D609), the intermediate key will be 4335 A065 CA4C 3CB5 03B1 A97D 6D66 543D.

2. The key corresponding to the trailing bits of 1010 (0x0A) is derived from the key for KSN 0x08. The intermediate key will be 44CD DFD1 AB03 8054 2CB5 07E7 7BD1 5B46.

3. The key corresponding to the trailing bits of 1011 (0x0B) is derived from the key above. The result will be 773F CDA4 4A97 6C4B 1123 CB29 4406 01DE.

D.4.3 Working key derivation

The working key derivation of the TDES DUKPT algorithm has two flavors. The PIN encryption key and the MAC keys are derived from the intermediate key by applying a variant. For instance, for the intermediate key above, 773F CDA4 4A97 6C4B 1123 CB29 4406 01DE, the PIN encryption key is obtained by XORing the last byte of each key half with 0xFF and would therefore be 773F CDA4 4A97 6CB4 1123 CB29 4406 0121.

The data key derivation process is different. In order to perform it, the intermediate key is first XORed with a variant (5th byte of each half key); for the example above, it will yield 773F CDA4 4A68 6C4B 1123 CB29 44F9 01DE. Then, the key is encrypted using itself as both the input block and the encryption key with the TDES algorithm in the ECB mode. The encryption yields BF38 43DD 414A F7FA 28BE 6BE3 5C33 BB19, which is then used as the data encryption key.

The example C implementation of some AES DUKPT functions can be found in src/dukpt.c.

D.5 AES DUKPT

D.5.1 Initial key derivation

The AES DUKPT standard supports many possible combinations of key algorithms. For the sake of simplicity, only AES 128-bit keys will be considered.

Let the BDK be DEAD BEEF 2233 4455 DEAD BEEF 2233 4455 DEAD BEEF, and let the KSN be 1234 5678 9012 3456 0000 0000. In order to derive the initial key from it, a derivation input vector is constructed as follows:

01 (version) 01 (counter) 8001 (key type) 0002 (algorithm) 0080 (length in bits) 1234 5678 9012 3456

The value is encrypted using the BDK with the AES algorithm to obtain the initial key of D10D D006 1E1A 580B C043 2D10 7219 D11B.

D.5.2 Intermediate key derivation

Assuming the initial key of D10D D006 1E1A 580B C043 2D10 7219 D11B and the KSN value of 1234 5678 9012 3456 0000 0001, the derivation input is constructed as follows:

01 (version) 01 (counter) 8000 (key type) 0002 (algorithm) 0080 (length in bits) 9012 3456 0000 0001.

It is encrypted using the initial key to yield 2904 AAA0 AD18 E574 F7F8 C389 527D 99C6.

For the transaction counter of 5, the derivation follows the pattern of TDES DUKPT. First, the key for KSN 4 is derived from the initial key:

$$K_4 = E_{IK}(123456789012345600000004) = 54C179DE23D9B01F219D7EDF2158927B$$

Then, the key for KSN 5 is derived from K_4:

$$K_5 = E_{K_4}(123456789012345600000005) = D318ACE3D42C812B2B9F7B379DDBDF7E.$$

The result is D318 ACE3 D42C 812B 2B9F 7B37 9DDB DF7E.

D.5.3 Working key derivation

As an example, consider the PIN encryption key. In order to derive it from the intermediate key above, the following input data vector is used:

01 (version) 01 (counter) 1000 (key type) 0002 (algorithm) 0080 (key length in bits) 9012 3456 0000 0005.

The PIN encryption key would be F309 2842 7D35 3BE7 614A DD0B A035 D012.

The example C implementation of some AES DUKPT functions can be found in src/dukpt.c.

Appendix E

JOSE Examples

E.1   JWE Example

Two examples of JWE calculation are provided in `bin/test_jose`: for the GCM method and the combination of AES encryption with SHA-256 HMAC.

With the latter, the method is as follows:

1. For a 256-bit CEK, its second half is used as the encryption key to encrypt the payload using AES-128 in the CBC mode.

2. AAD, the initialization vector, and the encrypted payload are concatenated.

3. 8-byte length of the AAD in bits in big-endian order is appended.

4. HMAC result is computed, using the first half of the CEK as the secret key and SHA-256 as the function.

5. he leading 128 bits of the HMAC output are used as the authentication tag.

The C implementation of the above computation can be found in `src/jose.c`, `jose_create_jwe()` function. The actual HMAC is computed in the `jose_encrypt_payload()` function.

DOI: 10.1201/9781003371366-E

Appendix F

Standard Bodies

Several major standard bodies affect the implementation of cryptography in payments. Some algorithms and methods are part of several standards from multiple organizations, while others have been withdrawn.

From a practical point of view, the availability of a standards document matters more than the nature of the organization that publishes it.

F.1 National Institution of Standards and Technology (NIST)

The National Institution of Standards and Technology is part of the United States Department of Commerce. It publishes and maintains Federal Information Processing Standards (FIPS). The publications are referred to as FIPS PUB xxx-yy, where xxx is the publication number and -yy is an optional revision number. A FIPS is intended for adoption by federal agencies.

Its Computer Security Resource Center publishes a series of Special Publications. The 800-series is dedicated to computer security and includes much of its outstanding cryptographic research. These publications are referred to as SP 800-xxRR, where xx is the publication number and RR refers to revision information either as a letter or as rN, where N is a number.

Both types of publications are available for free download from the NIST website [80].

F.2   American National Standards Institute (ANSI)

The American National Standards Institute is a private non-profit organization that oversees the development of voluntary standards for the United States. It is also the sole representative of the US in the International Organization for Standardization (ISO).

Its Accredited Standards Committee X9 (ASC X9) is an organization focused on developing standards for the financial services industry. It works closely with the ISO technical committee 68 (ISO/TC 68) with a similar focus.

The ASC X9 publishes standards relevant to the financial services industry, including data and information security. The ASC publications are referred to as ASC X9.xxx, where xxx is a number. The number can have parts and secondary standards suffixes in the form of -xxx and a suffix denoting the year of publication. The ASC also publishes technical reports, denoted ASC X9 TR xxx, where xxx is a number.

Most of the ASC standards are available for a fee from the ANSI web store, with a few being available for free [81].

F.3   International Organization for Standardization (ISO)

The International Organization for Standardization is an international standards organization comprised of representatives of national organizations from countries around the globe.

It has a joint technical committee with the International Electrotechnical Commission. The ISO has multiple technical subcommittees, including TC 68, responsible for the financial services industry. The ISO standards are referred to either as ISO xxxx:yyyy or ISO/IEC xxxx:yyyy, where xxxx is the standard number, yyyy may optionally specify the year of publication, and ISO/IEC indicates standards developed jointly with the IEC.

The ISO standards are available for a fee from the ISO website [82].

F.4   Internet Engineering Task Force (IETF)

The Internet Engineering Task Force (IETF) is a voluntary standards organization for the Internet with no formal membership.

The IETF publications are called "Request for Comments" (RFC) and are referred to as RFC xxxx, where xxxx is a number. Many standards are RFCs, but not all RFCs are standards.

The RFC publications are available for free from the IETF website [83].

F.5 International Telecommunication Union (ITU)

The International Telecommunication Union (ITU) is a specialized UN agency for global telecommunications. Its ITU Standardization sector, ITU-T, publishes Recommendations on various topics.

The data networks and security recommendations of the ITU-T are denoted with the prefix X and have the form of X.xxx, where xxx is a number.

The ITU-T recommendations are available for free from the ITU website [84].

F.6 EMVCo

Europay, Mastercard, and Visa originally formed EMVCo to develop secure technology that would combat card fraud. EMVCo is now owned by all major card schemes.

The technical body had initially focused on the EMV Chip specification. Contactless, mobile, and other relevant standards have been developed with time.

The EMV standard references differ depending on the standard.

The EMV specifications are available for free from the EMVCo website [48].

F.7 Payment Card Industry Security Standards Council (PCI SSC)

The Payment Card Industry Security Standards Council (PCI SSC) is a global standards organization that focuses on data security for payments.

The council is jointly owned by all major card schemes. It publishes standards and revisions for various aspects of data security.

The PCI SSC standard references differ depending on the standard.

The PCI SSC standard specifications are available for free from the PCI SSC website [85].

References

[1] International Committee for Information Technology Standards (INCITS). Data Encryption Algorithm. Standard ANSI X3.92-1981, American National Standards Institute, Maryland, USA, 1998.

[2] National Institute of Standards and Technology. Data Encryption Standard (DES). Technical Report Federal Information Processing Standards Publications (FIPS PUBS) 46-3, U.S. Department of Commerce, Washington, D.C., 1999.

[3] ISO Central Secretary. Banking – Personal Identification Number management and security – Part 2: Approved algorithm(s) for PIN encipherment. Standard ISO 9564-2:1991, International Organization for Standardization, Geneva, CH, 1991.

[4] National Institute of Standards and Technology. Advanced Encryption Standard (AES). Technical Report Federal Information Processing Standards Publications (FIPS PUBS) 197, U.S. Department of Commerce, Washington, D.C., 2001.

[5] ISO Central Secretary. Information technology – Security techniques – Encryption algorithms – Part 3: Block ciphers. Standard ISO/IEC 18033-3:2010, International Organization for Standardization, Geneva, CH, 2010.

[6] Ronald L. Rivest, Leonard M. Adleman, and Adi Shamir. Cryptographic communications system and method, Sep 1983.

[7] Wikipedia. RSA (cryptosystem) — Wikipedia, the free encyclopedia. https://en.wikipedia.org/wiki/RSA_(cryptosystem), 2022.

[8] Kathleen Moriarty, Burt Kaliski, Jakob Jonsson, and Andreas Rusch. PKCS #1: RSA Cryptography Specifications Version 2.2. RFC 8017, November 2016.

[9] Wikipedia. Diffie–Hellman key exchange — Wikipedia, the free encyclopedia. https://en.wikipedia.org/wiki/Diffie%E2%80%93Hellman_key_exchange, 2022.

[10] Eric Rescorla. Diffie-Hellman Key Agreement Method. RFC 2631, June 1999.

[11] Arjen K. Lenstra and Eric R. Verheul. Selecting Cryptographic Key Sizes. In Hideki Imai and Yuliang Zheng, editors, *Public Key Cryptography*, pages 446–465, Berlin, Heidelberg, 2000. Springer Berlin Heidelberg.

[12] National Institute of Standards and Technology. Digital Signature Standard (DSS). Technical Report Federal Information Processing Standards Publications (FIPS PUBS) 186-4, U.S. Department of Commerce, Washington, D.C., 2013.

[13] National Institute of Standards and Technology. Recommendation for pairwise key-establishment schemes using discrete logarithm cryptography. Technical Report NIST Special Publication 800-56A Revision 3, U.S. Department of Commerce, Washington, D.C., 2018.

[14] Ronald L. Rivest. The MD5 Message-Digest Algorithm. RFC 1321, April 1992.

[15] National Institute of Standards and Technology. Secure Hash Standard (SHS). Technical Report Federal Information Processing Standards Publications (FIPS PUBS) 180-4, U.S. Department of Commerce, Washington, D.C., 2015.

[16] National Institute of Standards and Technology. SHA-3 Standard: Permutation-Based Hash and Extendable-Output Functions. Technical Report Federal Information Processing Standards Publications (FIPS PUBS) 202, U.S. Department of Commerce, Washington, D.C., 2015.

[17] ISO Central Secretary. Information technology – Security techniques – Message Authentication Codes (MACs) – Part 1: Mechanisms using a block cipher. Standard ISO/IEC 9797-1:2011, International Organization for Standardization, Geneva, CH, 2011.

[18] Walter Tuchman. Iv. 'Hellman presents no shortcut solutions to the DES'. *IEEE Spectrum*, 16(7):40–41, 1979.

[19] Phil R. Karn, William A. Simpson, and Perry E. Metzger. The ESP Triple DES Transform. RFC 1851, September 1995.

[20] Thai Duong and Juliano Rizzo. Flickr's API signature forgery vulnerability, Sep 2009.

[21] Wikipedia. Length extension attack — Wikipedia, the free encyclopedia. https://en.wikipedia.org/wiki/Length_extension_attack, 2022. [Online; accessed 01-July-2022].

[22] ISO Central Secretary. Information technology – Security techniques – Message Authentication Codes (MACs) – Part 2: Mechanisms using a dedicated hash-function. Standard ISO/IEC 9797-2:2021, International Organization for Standardization, Geneva, CH, 2021.

[23] ISO Central Secretary. Information technology – Security techniques – Message Authentication Codes (MACs) – Part 3: Mechanisms using a universal hash-function. Standard ISO/IEC 9797-3:2011, International Organization for Standardization, Geneva, CH, 2011.

[24] Dr. Hugo Krawczyk, Mihir Bellare, and Ran Canetti. HMAC: Keyed-Hashing for Message Authentication. RFC 2104, February 1997.

[25] National Institute of Standards and Technology. Digital Signature Standard (DSS). Technical Report Federal Information Processing Standards Publications (FIPS PUBS) 186-1, U.S. Department of Commerce, Washington, D.C., 1998.

[26] National Institute of Standards and Technology. Recommendation for block cipher modes of operation: Galois/counter mode (gcm) and gmac. Technical Report NIST Special Publication 800-38D, U.S. Department of Commerce, Washington, D.C., 2007.

[27] National Institute of Standards and Technology. Recommendation for key derivation using pseudorandom functions (revised). Technical Report NIST Special Publication 800-108, U.S. Department of Commerce, Washington, D.C., 2009.

[28] National Institute of Standards and Technology. Recommendation for block cipher modes of operation: The cmac mode for authentication. Technical Report NIST Special Publication 800-38B, U.S. Department of Commerce, Washington, D.C., 2005.

[29] National Institute of Standards and Technology. Recommendation for pairwise key establishment schemes using discrete logarithm cryptography. Technical Report NIST Special Publication 800-56A, U.S. Department of Commerce, Washington, D.C., 2008.

[30] Telecommunication Standardization Sector of ITU. Information technology – Open Systems Interconnection – The Directory: Public-key and attribute certificate frameworks. Technical Report X.509, International Telecommunication Union, Geneva, CH, 2019.

[31] ISO Central Secretary. Information technology – Open Systems Interconnection – The Directory – Part 8: Public-key and attribute certificate frameworks. Standard ISO/IEC 9594-8:2014, International Organization for Standardization, Geneva, CH, 2014.

[32] Magnus Nystrom and Burt Kaliski. PKCS #10: Certification Request Syntax Specification Version 1.7. RFC 2986, November 2000.

[33] Kathleen Moriarty, Magnus Nystrom, Sean Parkinson, Andreas Rusch, and Michael Scott. PKCS #12: Personal Information Exchange Syntax v1.1. RFC 7292, July 2014.

[34] Russ Housley. Cryptographic Message Syntax (CMS). RFC 5652, September 2009.

[35] Stefan Santesson, Michael Myers, Rich Ankney, Ambarish Malpani, Slava Galperin, and Dr. Carlisle Adams. X.509 Internet Public Key Infrastructure Online Certificate Status Protocol – OCSP. RFC 6960, June 2013.

[36] Telecommunication Standardization Sector of ITU. Information technology – Abstract Syntax Notation one (ASN.1): Specification of basic notation. Technical Report X.680, International Telecommunication Union, Geneva, CH, 2021.

[37] Telecommunication Standardization Sector of ITU. Information technology – Abstract Syntax Notation One (ASN.1): Information object specification. Technical Report X.681, International Telecommunication Union, Geneva, CH, 2021.

[38] Telecommunication Standardization Sector of ITU. Information technology – Abstract Syntax Notation One (ASN.1): Constraint specification. Technical Report X.682, International Telecommunication Union, Geneva, CH, 2021.

[39] Telecommunication Standardization Sector of ITU. Information technology – Abstract Syntax Notation One (ASN.1): Parameterization of ASN.1 specifications. Technical Report X.683, International Telecommunication Union, Geneva, CH, 2021.

[40] Telecommunication Standardization Sector of ITU. Information technology – ASN.1 encoding rules: Specification of Basic Encoding Rules (BER), Canonical Encoding Rules (CER) and Distinguished Encoding Rules (DER). Technical Report X.690, International Telecommunication Union, Geneva, CH, 2021.

[41] Telecommunication Standardization Sector of ITU. Information technology – ASN.1 encoding rules: Specification of Packed Encoding Rules

(PER). Technical Report X.691, International Telecommunication Union, Geneva, CH, 2021.

[42] Telecommunication Standardization Sector of ITU. Information technology – ASN.1 encoding rules: Specification of Encoding Control Notation (ECN). Technical Report X.692, International Telecommunication Union, Geneva, CH, 2021.

[43] Telecommunication Standardization Sector of ITU. Information technology – ASN.1 encoding rules: XML Encoding Rules (XER). Technical Report X.693, International Telecommunication Union, Geneva, CH, 2021.

[44] Telecommunication Standardization Sector of ITU. Information technology – ASN.1 encoding rules: Mapping W3C XML schema definitions into ASN.1. Technical Report X.694, International Telecommunication Union, Geneva, CH, 2021.

[45] Telecommunication Standardization Sector of ITU. Information technology – ASN.1 encoding rules: Registration and application of PER encoding instructions. Technical Report X.695, International Telecommunication Union, Geneva, CH, 2021.

[46] Telecommunication Standardization Sector of ITU. Information technology – ASN.1 encoding rules: Specification of Octet Encoding Rules (OER). Technical Report X.696, International Telecommunication Union, Geneva, CH, 2021.

[47] I. Dubinsky. *Acquiring Card Payments*. Auerbach Publications, 1 edition, September 2019.

[48] EMVCo. https://www.emvco.com/.

[49] ISO Central Secretary. Identification cards – Recording technique. Standard ISO/IEC 7811, International Organization for Standardization, Geneva, CH, 2018.

[50] ISO Central Secretary. Information technology – Identification cards - Financial transaction cards. Standard ISO/IEC 7813:2006, International Organization for Standardization, Geneva, CH, 2006.

[51] ISO Central Secretary. Identification cards – Financial transaction cards – Magnetic stripe data content for track 3. Standard ISO/IEC 4909:2006, International Organization for Standardization, Geneva, CH, 2006.

[52] EMVCo. EMV Integrated Circuit Card Specifications for Payment Systems – Book 1 – Application Independent ICC to Terminal Interface Requirements. Standard 4.3, EMVCo, 2011.

[53] EMVCo. EMV Integrated Circuit Card Specifications for Payment Systems – Book 2 – Security and Key Management. Standard 4.3, EMVCo, 2011.

[54] EMVCo. EMV Integrated Circuit Card Specifications for Payment Systems – Book 3 – Application Specification. Standard 4.3, EMVCo, 2011.

[55] EMVCo. EMV Integrated Circuit Card Specifications for Payment Systems – Book 4 – Cardholder, Attendant, and Acquirer Interface Requirements. Standard 4.3, EMVCo, 2011.

[56] ISO Central Secretary. Financial services – Personal Identification number (PIN) management and security – Part 1: Basic principles and requirements for PINs in card-based systems. Standard ISO 9564-1:2017, International Organization for Standardization, Geneva, CH, 2017.

[57] Transport Layer Security (TLS) Extensions. https://www.iana.org/assignments/tls- extensiontype-values/tls-extensiontype-values.xhtml.

[58] Telecommunication Standardization Sector of ITU. X.501 : Information technology – Open Systems Interconnection – The Directory: Models. Technical Report X.501, International Telecommunication Union, Geneva, CH, 2019.

[59] Tim Bray. The JavaScript Object Notation (JSON) Data Interchange Format. RFC 8259, December 2017.

[60] Michael Jones and Joe Hildebrand. JSON Web Encryption (JWE). RFC 7516, May 2015.

[61] Michael Jones, John Bradley, and Nat Sakimura. JSON Web Signature (JWS). RFC 7515, May 2015.

[62] Michael Jones. JSON Web Algorithms (JWA). RFC 7518, May 2015.

[63] Michael Jones. JSON Web Key (JWK). RFC 7517, May 2015.

[64] JSON Web Signature and Encryption Algorithms. https://www.iana.org/assignments/jose/jose.xhtml#web-signature-encryption-algorithms.

[65] JSON Web Key Elliptic Curve. https://www.iana.org/assignments/jose/jose.xhtml#web-key-elliptic-curve.

[66] EMVCo. EMV 3-D Secure – Protocol and Core Functions Specification. Standard 2.3.0.0, EMVCo, 2021.

[67] Accredited Standards Committee X9-Financial Services. Financial Institution Key Management (Wholesale). Standard ANSI X9.17-1985, American National Standards Institute, Maryland, USA, 1985.

[68] Accredited Standards Committee X9-Financial Services. Interoperable Secure Key Exchange Key Block Specification. Standard ASC X9 TR 31-2018, American National Standards Institute, Maryland, USA, 2018.

[69] National Institute of Standards and Technology. Recommendation for Existing Application-Specific Key Derivation Functions. Technical Report NIST Special Publication 800-135, U.S. Department of Commerce, Washington, D.C., 2011.

[70] Accredited Standards Committee X9-Financial Services. Retail Financial Services – Symmetric Key Management – Part 3: Derived Unique Key Per Transaction. Standard ANSI X9.24-3-2017, American National Standards Institute, Maryland, USA, 2017.

[71] The European Union and Commission. DIRECTIVE (EU) 2015/2366 OF THE EUROPEAN PARLIAMENT AND OF THE COUNCIL. *Official Journal of the European Union*, page 35, December 2015.

[72] National Institute of Standards and Technology. A Statistical Test Suite for Random and Pseudorandom Number Generators for Cryptographic Applications. Technical Report NIST Special Publication 800-22, U.S. Department of Commerce, Washington, D.C., 2010.

[73] Wikipedia. The Gold-Bug – Wikipedia, the free encyclopedia. https://en.wikipedia.org/wiki/The_Gold-Bug, 2022. [Online; accessed 05-July-2022].

[74] Bit Twiddling Hacks. http://www.graphics.stanford.edu/šeander/bithacks.html.

[75] ISO Central Secretary. Identification cards – Identification of issuers – Part 1: Numbering system. Standard ISO/IEC 7812-1:2017, International Organization for Standardization, Geneva, CH, 2017.

[76] Ned Freed and Dr. Nathaniel S. Borenstein. Multipurpose Internet Mail Extensions (MIME) Part One: Format of Internet Message Bodies. RFC 2045, November 1996.

[77] Simon Josefsson. The Base16, Base32, and Base64 Data Encodings. RFC 4648, October 2006.

[78] OpenSSL Cryptography and SSL/TLS Toolkit. https://www.openssl.org/.

[79] Shamir's Secret Sharing Scheme. http://point-at-infinity.org/ssss/.

[80] National Institution of Standards and Technology. https://www.nist.gov/.

[81] ANSI Webstore. https://webstore.ansi.org/.

[82] International Organization for Standardization. https://www.iso.org/.

[83] Publishing and accessing RFCs. https://www.ietf.org/standards/publication/.

[84] ITU. https://www.itu.int/en/Pages/default.aspx.

[85] PCI Security Standards Council. https://www.pcisecuritystandards.org/.

Index

Printed in the United States
by Baker & Taylor Publisher Services